TAKING CHARGE

Perry M. Smith

TAKING CHARGE
A Practical Guide for Leaders

Introduction by James Bond Stockdale

1986
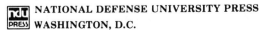 NATIONAL DEFENSE UNIVERSITY PRESS
WASHINGTON, D.C.

NATIONAL DEFENSE UNIVERSITY PRESS PUBLICATIONS

To increase general knowledge and inform discussion, NDU Press publishes books on subjects relating to US national security.

Each year, the National Defense University, through the Institute for National Strategic Studies, hosts about two dozen Senior Fellows who engage in original research on national security issues. NDU Press publishes the best of this research.

In addition, the Press publishes other especially timely or distinguished writing on national security, as well as new editions of out-of-print defense classics, and books based on University-sponsored conferences concerning national security affairs.

Library of Congress Cataloging-in-Publication Data

Smith, Perry M. (Perry McCoy)
    Taking Charge.

    Bibliography: p. 221
    Includes index.
    1. Leadership.   2. Decision-making.   3. Communication
in organizations.   4. Command of troops.   1. Title.
HM141.S62   1986   303.3'4   86–18014

Editorial Research Associates, of Washington, DC, copymarked and proofread this book under contract DAHC32–86–A–0002.

Editorial Experts, Inc. of Alexandria, Virginia, indexed this book under contract DAHC32–86–A–0009.

William A. Palmer, Jr., of Cheltenham, Maryland, read final page proofs under contract DAHC32-86-A-0005.

NDU Press publications are sold by the US Government Printing Office. For ordering information, call (202) 783-3238 or write to Superintendent of Documents, US Government Printing Office, Washington, DC 20402.

First printing, September 1986
Third printing, August 1987
Fifth printing, January 1989
Seventh printing, July 1992

Second printing, April 1987
Fourth printing, April 1988
Sixth printing, July 1990
Eighth printing, November 1993

In memory of General Jerry O'Malley, United States Air Force, who, in his distinguished career, taught many thousands in all the military services so much about leadership.

CONTENTS

FOREWORD

Major General Smith's fundamental premise in writing *Taking Charge* is that leaders count, that leaders can—*should*—make a difference in the organizations they head up. Successful leaders, those who make a difference, seem to share certain personal characteristics and leadership strategies. However, despite shared traits such as vision and intuition and methods such as delegation and feedback, all leaders are not necessarily ready to run large and complex organizations, like an Air Force wing, an Army division, or an embassy. Thus the author proposes this essential corollary to his premise that leaders count: *large and complex organizations make special demands on the men and women who run them.* To help those with the special task of leading such organizations, General Smith presents, in a well organized fashion, soundly tested, practical advice for middle and senior managers.

Taking Charge is a particularly accessible book: one that leaders will want to keep handy for reference. General Smith's conversational, anecdotal writing style is enriched by useable checklists and germane case studies. His book brings the art of leadership down to earth and into the hands of working leaders—a goal the National Defense University is pleased to support.

RICHARD D. LAWRENCE
Lieutenant General, US Army
President, National Defense
    University

ACKNOWLEDGMENTS

To enrich a leadership course I taught at the National War College, I invited many guest speakers. I am indebted to them for their insights.

In particular, I would like to thank John Gardner; Ambassador Bill Harrop, the Inspector General of the State Department; Secretary of the Air Force Verne Orr; Lieutenant General Bob Springer, USAF; Lieutenant General Walt Ulmer, USA (Ret); General Bill Dupuy, USA (Ret); Lieutenant General Bill Maloney, USMC; Mr. Tom Pownall, Chief Executive Officer, Martin–Marietta; General Bob Russ, USAF; Mr. Bob Kirk, President, LTV Aerospace; and Vice Admiral James Stockdale, USN (Ret).

Special thanks are due Mary McNabb who took dictation by the hour; Yvette Taylor of the National Defense University who typed the initial manuscript without complaint; Patricia Pasquaret who took over the typing and editing duties; Lieutenant Junior Grade Cathy Salvato, USN, who accomplished many editorial chores; Sherwood (Woody) Goldberg, who helped restructure the manuscript at a critical phase; Colonel Jack Jacobs, USA; Captain Mike Miller, USN; Major General Charles Hamm, USAF; Jane Hamm; Brigadier General Bob Plowden, USAF; Harriet Plowden; Vice Admiral James Stockdale; Colonel Edward B. Parks, USAF; Lieutenant Colonel William H. Clover, USAF; and Lieutenant Colonel Jim Simms, USA, for their substantive and editorial comments.

And, to my wife, Connor Smith, who edited, critiqued, and put up with a husband once again inspired to write.

PREFACE

The purpose of this book is to provide a practical guide for leaders who head large and complex organizations.

My fundamental premise is that leaders count, that people at the top can—should—make a difference. By setting standards, goals, and priorities, by establishing and nurturing a network of communications, a leader can make a difference in the daily performance of an organization. A leader can permanently affect an organization by establishing a strategic vision and setting long-term goals.

Leadership skills can be improved by reading, discussion, use of case studies, and wrestling with concepts. By learning from mistakes of others and by thinking through leadership problems and issues, leaders will be better prepared to face most challenges.

The future is *not* already determined. What will happen in the next twenty or thirty years is, in large part, the consequence of decisions that leaders will make within government and within their own organizations. It is no exaggeration that leaders of institutions in the Western world do and will shape the future of their nations and the world.

For the purpose of this book, I define large organizations as those with more than one thousand people under the command of a single individual, such as an Air Force wing, an Army brigade, or a large ship. I see complex organizations as organizations of one hundred or more individuals, but organizations which have such diverse or complex responsibilities that the leader is unable to keep track of all the ongoing issues at one time. Examples might be large embassies or large staff directorates.

Leading large and complex organizations requires an approach different from those used in leading smaller organizations. For instance, in large and complex organizations, leaders may not personally know all of their subordinates. Leaders can no longer be specific problem solvers. Communication to the lower echelons becomes much more difficult, and feedback returns through several layers. The intimidation factor of being the "big boss" can impede good communication in both directions. The tendency for the leader to make superficial judgments about the capabilities of individuals tends to increase. Sycophants, who tend to isolate the leader from the important issues or who fail to challenge the leader when he has a bad idea, are generally more prevalent in large organizations than in small ones. The leader of a large organization has a more difficult and larger role to train other leaders. Greater delegation, trust, empowerment, and loyalty to subordinate leaders are also all at play.

As Commandant of the National War College, I have had a luxury few leaders enjoy—the luxury of time: time for reflection, time for teaching, time for research, and time for writing. Teaching an elective course exposed me to the insights of 136 students from the Industrial College of the Armed Forces, from a number of National Defense University International Fellows, and from the National War College. Most of these students had already led sizeable organizations. They wrote papers, participated actively in a seminar environment, challenged my views, and forced me to revisit, in greater depth, my own experiences as a leader.

The case studies outlined in Appendix B are the product of personal experience or the experiences of leaders I know. Mistakes, personal as they may be, are shared so that the reader might learn and perhaps avoid similar circumstances and errors.

PERRY M. SMITH
MAJOR GENERAL, US AIR FORCE
COMMANDANT, NATIONAL WAR COLLEGE
WASHINGTON, DC

INTRODUCTION

by James Bond Stockdale

Leaders who run large organizations face an enormous challenge. They are responsible for the lives, welfare, and morale of the people, while at the same time they must ensure that the organizational goals and missions are well served. Major General Perry M. Smith has written, with wit and wisdom, a book which should be most helpful to both leaders of today and those who will move into leadership positions in future years.

Although there are a great number of excellent works on the subject of leadership, this book fills an important void. It is just what it says it is—a practical guide to leadership. Through the use of case studies, checklists, helpful hints, rules of thumb, and other techniques, this book has a feel of relevance and pragmatism, while, at the same time, it helps the leader set standards of excellence and high integrity. The reader should find particularly intriguing such insights as the "Four-Hour in the Office

Rule," the "Sixty Percent" Decision Rule, the "Skeleton in the Closet" Question, the "Oh, by the way" Dilemma, the "No Nonconcurrence through Silence" Policy, the "One Push" rule of sponsorship, "bonding" techniques, "dignity checks," and other helpful hints. In addition, the discussion of opportunity planning, integrity reinforcement, divestiture strategies, soft and hard firings, creative compliments, protecting the leader's signature, velocity of innovation, institutional integrity, self-abnegation, ad-hocracy, and the small nation syndrome in international organizations are most useful.

I had the pleasure of assisting General Smith when he taught a leadership course at the National Defense University. These students, from both the Industrial College of the Armed Forces and the National War College, are the best mid-level professionals that this country produces. They also contributed a great deal to the course by sharing their leadership experiences in the five military services and in many federal agencies. *Taking Charge* is, therefore, much more than the insights Perry Smith has collected in his numerous leadership jobs in operational units, international staffs, planning staffs, and academic institutions. *Taking Charge* benefits considerably from inputs of 136 mature and experienced students, in their writings and in their classroom discussions, over the past three years.

An additional advantage of this book is that the author gets right to the point and writes in a crisp and clear style. Leaders will want to have *Taking Charge* on their desks so that they can refer to it periodically when they have to face tough problems or difficult decisions on hiring, firing, counselling, planning, etc. His case studies raise many important issues. By putting them in a separate appendix, by sticking to real life occurrences that actually happened to him or his colleagues, by explaining how each case was handled, and by critiquing the approaches taken, the author maximizes the value of these leadership vignettes. Finally, the checklists contained in Appendix A should get lots of usage by leaders. They provide quick reminders in such key areas as introspection, decisionmaking, and communications.

But there is still another reason why this is a valuable book: its messages jump out at the reader, not only because they are unmistakably authentic, coming from the mind of a man who has been there himself, but because they also come from the pen of a natural teacher. Perry Smith has a feel for what kind of questions will arise in the minds of his audience and answers them as he goes along. Major General Smith was a "teaching" Commandant of the National War College who could regularly be found in front of a classroom explaining complex things in simple understandable terms to genuinely interested listeners. He is a master of the art of explanation, which means he is also a master of the art of teaching, which almost always means, as it does in this case, that he is a natural leader as well.

TAKING CHARGE

1/LEADING:
twenty fundamentals to remember

THERE ARE TWENTY KEY fundamentals that form the basis for this philosophy of leadership. While some of these fundamentals will be discussed in greater detail later in this book, they are presented here to help the reader understand the foundations of my thinking on leadership of large organizations.

1. *Trust Is Vital.* If you lead a large organization, it is essential to be able to trust your subordinate leaders. Such trust is difficult for some leaders who want to direct every aspect of their organization. These leaders cannot find their way clear to trust people and, as a result, they do not nurture subleaders or give them the opportunity to exercise their full creative talents. To be a truly effective leader, particularly of a large organization, requires a great deal of trust in one's subordinates. This trust

3

needs to be balanced with a willingness to remove people who cannot be trusted, and to make some tough decisions. Without trust and mutual respect among leaders and subordinate leaders, a large organization will often suffer a combination of low performance and poor morale. In the words of Frank Crane, "You may be deceived if you trust too much, but you will live in torment if you do not trust enough."

2. *A Leader Must Be a Good Teacher.* Teachership and leadership go hand-in-glove. The leader must be willing to teach skills, to share insights and experiences, and to work very closely with people to help them mature and be creative. In order to be a good teacher, a leader has to be a good communicator, must be well organized and a goal-setter. By teaching, leaders can inspire, motivate, and influence subordinates at various levels.

3. *A Leader Should Rarely Be a Problem Solver.* A leader should facilitate problem solving, but should let subordinates solve most problems. The psychic reward that a subordinate gets from actually solving problems is quite important. It builds self-esteem and enhances the subordinate's ability to do still better in subsequent situations. Even though the leader can often solve the problem more quickly than subordinates, it is poor practice to be the problem solver. There are, of course, occasional exceptions to this rule. At times when the organization is in serious trouble, when subordinates appear unable to formulate a good answer to a problem, when only the leader has the expertise, the understanding, or the contacts to make the right decisions, the leader

should step in. By being the problem solver of last resort, the leader can help the organization grow and thrive. General George Patton advised: "Never tell people how to do things. Tell them what to do and they will surprise you with their ingenuity."

4. *A Leader Must Be a Communicator.* If a leader is a good writer, communications, both up and down the organizational structure, will occur in a way that is meaningful, understandable, and has impact. If a good editor, the leader can work on papers, issues, and problems that come in written form to make sure they are clearly and simply stated so that they can have the maximum positive impact. If a good speaker, the leader can "reach out," make people feel good about themselves and take pride in their work. If a good listener, the leader can accept ideas, criticism, and other feedback that can improve the organization and create an atmosphere of excellence and caring. In the words of an unknown sage, "I never learned anything while I was talking." A dynamic communicator can motivate people to want to go back to work, committed to doing an even better job than they did in the past.

5. *A Leader Must Manage Time Well and Use It Effectively.* A leader who knows how to dictate clearly to secretaries and to dictating machines can save precious time. Teddy Roosevelt was able to dictate as many as twenty-five letters an hour. (He would alternate back and forth between two secretaries.) He was able to complete most of a full day's work in a couple of hours through this dictation method. Fast and efficient dictation, of course, requires a secretary who can take dictation well and a leader

5

who can organize thoughts effectively so that spoken words turn into written words rather easily.

Another aspect of managing time is speed reading. Time can be better utilized if a leader can read very fast and pick up the essence of issues rapidly. Speed reading courses, or just the practice of reading fast, is very helpful. If a leader can get through an "in-box" in an hour or two, whereas it might take a slower reader a full day, more time will be available to be out with people, to have substantive meetings on important issues and to be a true leader, rather than just a desk manager.

A third aspect of time management involves the maximum use of executive secretaries, administrative and special assistants, or deputies. Recruiting, testing, and hiring in this area is vitally important. A good executive secretary can help you manage your time well and watch your calendar carefully to make sure that the calendar reflects how you want to spend your day. Working very carefully with an executive secretary to work out a weekly or monthly schedule that fits your time clock, your body rhythms, and your priorities is an important aspect of time management.

Another one is maintaining "open time" every day. Open time should be for thinking, dealing with crises, seeing unexpected visitors, or dealing with fast moving issues. If your calendar is filled from 7:30 a.m. until 6:00 p.m., at fifteen or thirty minute intervals, you are poorly managing your time. You are probably getting into too much detail and not allowing yourself time to think. Subordinates who really need to see you may not reach you promptly.

As a general rule, a leader should not schedule more than one event an hour. A meeting with an individual, the corporate staff, one of your divisions, and other meetings should be scheduled in such a way that you will have time at the end of each before the next event takes place. In between these meetings, throughout the day, you should have time to return phone calls, work on items in your in-box, and to think and prepare for the next meeting. It is a reality of leading a large organization that there are increasing demands on your time. More and more people want and need to see you. Organizational priorities and your own priorities come into conflict. Leaders must work smarter, not harder, must learn to say "no" to time wasters, and must deal with the pathology of information and information overload. The key is to understand that as the leader, you can manage your time, but it takes work, self-discipline, and planning.

6. *Leaders Should Trust Their Intuition.* Leaders probably would not have reached their present positions unless they had good intuition. They should continue to trust that intuition. Are they satisfied with the decisions they have made? Are the decisions others have made acceptable? Does something seem wrong? These are the kinds of questions that they should ask themselves. If their intuition sends them signals that would indicate the organization may be going in the wrong direction, they should respond, raise some additional questions, and postpone important decisions until they are reasonably comfortable that they are choosing the right course. To quote Ralph Waldo Emerson: "The essence of

genius is spontaneity and instinct. Trust thyself." Part of intuition is having your "antennae" out, keeping your hand on the pulse of the organization, and being "street smart" and "in touch."

7. *Leaders Must Be Willing to Remove People for Cause.* The leader is responsible for ensuring that the mission is accomplished. Inhibitors to this task, such as the continued presence of ineffective subordinates, drain the organization and its capable leaders of the time, energy, and attention needed to accomplish the mission. In such circumstances, leaders have a responsibility to the organization to remove those who stand in the way of success. Leaders are not serving themselves well; they're not serving the institution well; and, in many cases, they're not serving the incompetent individuals well by keeping them on in responsible positions. Leaders should remove people in key positions personally. The removal should be done with grace and style, but also with firmness. When you call individuals in to ask them to move on, you should be willing to do so and not end the meeting unable to get to the point.

8. *Leaders Must Take Care of Their People.* Leaders should work to get good assignments or jobs for deserving individuals when those people leave the organization. Leaders should *never* ask subordinates to write their own personal evaluations or effectiveness reports; leaders should write or edit the effectiveness reports or their personal evaluations and make sure that these are done with care, and style. Leaders should get up in the morning thanking people; at noontime they should thank more people; before going home at night, they should thank still more.

8

Thanking people is an important part of taking care of them because it's taking care of their psychological health. Leaders should sponsor outstanding subordinates while avoiding the pitfalls of cronyism. They should follow Pierce Chapron's advice when he helps people: "He who receives a benefit should never forget it; he who bestows should never remember it."

9. *Leaders Must Provide Vision.* Leaders who are not planners are simply caretakers and gatekeepers. Though they may run efficient and effective organizations, they do not really serve the long-term interests of the institution unless they plan, set goals, and provide strategic vision. Leaders who care about their missions and about their people normally want to leave their organizations in better shape and with a clearer strategic direction than when they took over. Good planning, goal setting, and priority setting can accomplish these things and create a marvelous legacy.

10. *Leaders Must Subordinate Their Ambitions and Egos to the Goals of the Unit or the Institution That They Lead.* Often leaders have to subvert their strong personal ambition in order to ensure that the development and maturation of their organizations and the movement towards higher standards of excellence and performance are accomplished in a careful and systematic way. The selfless leader gains the respect of subordinates and the support of superiors. If leaders are too ambitious for the organization, or too ambitious for themselves, they may drive the organization in dysfunctional directions. They may, in

fact, become a part of the problem rather than a part of the solution.

11. *Leaders Must Know How to Run Meetings.* Much of a leader's time is spent in meetings. Leaders should know what kind of meetings they're attending; they should establish the ground rules for the meetings; they should be actively involved in the meetings to make sure they stay on track; they should give individuals ample opportunity to express their views and their disagreements. Finally, leaders should know how to wrap up meetings, to draw conclusions, to set up the time and agenda for the next meeting on the subject, and to direct individuals in the meeting to carry out certain tasks as a result of the decisions that have been made. Leaders also must discontinue regular (weekly, monthly, quarterly) meetings which are not serving an important purpose. American leaders especially must fight the cultural tendency to hold long, undisciplined meetings with little useful output.

12. *Leaders Must Understand the Decisionmaking and Implementation Processes.* How are decisions made? How do leaders want to make decisions? Which decisions do they want subordinates to make? How much control do they have over decisions? What decisions do they have to get approved by higher authority? These are the sort of questions leaders should be able to answer. Leaders also must understand how to implement decisions. Decisions made are of little value if they are not implemented, so leaders must know how to develop implementing strategies. They must have follow-up systems to

ensure that decisions are not only carried out, but carried out faithfully, in both substance and spirit.

13. *Leaders Must Be Visible and Approachable.* In large organizations, the four-hour rule is a useful guide: Leaders should spend no more than four hours a day in their offices. The rest of the time they should be out with their people, conducting meetings, and visiting subordinates in their work areas. They should be talking to lower level officials and getting their feedback on problem areas. They should be patting people on the back. They should be making short speeches. They should be handing out awards. They should be traveling widely throughout their organizations. They should be making contact with sister organizations and organizations at higher levels so they can ensure that important relationships are enhanced and problem areas identified early. When they are having meetings or discussions in their offices, they should never sit behind their desks, but should go to a couch or sofa and get away from an imposing position which is often intimidating to subordinates. To make visitors feel comfortable, leaders should sit in the more sociable areas of their offices, close the door, and make the individual think that nothing else matters except the subject the subordinate brings to the leader.

Another aspect of being approachable is getting involved in sports, hobbies, little theater groups, social gatherings, religious activities, etc., so that leaders can be out with subordinates, having contact with them at various levels. If, for instance, a leader jogs with subordinates, all kinds of interesting things that are going on in an organization may be discovered. A lower level subordinate usually will be more frank on a jogging trail than in an office. Company or unit softball leagues, basketball programs, tennis matches, or volleyball competitions serve the same purpose. A leader often can find out more about what's going on in a sporting or social atmosphere than in the front office. People will feel more comfortable if they see their leader in all kinds of different contexts: social, athletic, business, religious, personal, and so forth. Be benignly visible; be approachably visible. Some people are very visible but not approachable. One caution in this regard is appropriate: a "just-one-of-the-guys" kind of person is normally not a good leader. A leader must be special while being approachable.

14. *Leaders Should Have a Sense of Humor.* Most of the time, leaders should laugh at themselves rather than at others. They should generally be willing to tell jokes or even embarrassing stories about their own mistakes to let people know that they are human, that they err, and that they are willing to admit errors. They should let people know that life is not so important that you can't sit back occasionally and be amused by what's happening. Humor can be a great reliever of tension; a story or a joke at times of crisis or difficulty can be very therapeutic. Be relaxed, be humorous with people, but don't use humor against people. Humor, delivered with an acid tongue and aimed at subordinates, can be very counterproductive.

15. *Leaders Must Be Decisive, but Patiently Decisive.* Leaders should listen to all sides before

deciding. They should, on occasion, postpone an important decision for a day or two, or even a week or two, while collecting additional information. However, a leader must be decisive. Institutions and organizations need decisions. Yet, they need a leader who is patiently decisive, who doesn't jump as soon as the first individual comes in and makes a recommendation for a decision. A leader should always look for contrasting views. If at all possible, sleep on important issues. Leaders should talk to their executive officers, deputies, spouses, or other people who can be trusted to forgo personal or parochial interests. A leader also should talk to people who may not like the tentative decision to find out what their opposing views might be. However, postponing the decision for weeks or months is rarely the answer. A non-decision is itself a decision and should be recognized for what it is. Risk taking is frequently an essential and healthy aspect of decisionmaking.

16. *Leaders Should Be Introspective.* Leaders should be able to look at themselves objectively and analyze where they have made mistakes, where they've turned off people and where they've headed down the wrong path. They must be able to look in the mirror and determine what they did right today, what they did wrong today, what decisions they need to go back to again, and how approachable they were. They should ask themselves if they have been too cooped up, too narrow, or too rigid. Introspection can be followed to a fault, however. Hamlets make poor leaders.

17. *Leaders Should Be Reliable.* A leader should be careful about what commitments are made, but once those commitments are firm, nothing short of major health problems or a very serious crisis in business, institution, or family matters should alter them. Reliability is something that leaders must have in order to provide stability and strength to organizations. Important aspects of reliability are persistence and consistency. Leaders must be willing to be flexible, but consistency and coherence are important elements of large organizations and deserve the support of top leaders.

18. *Leaders Should Be Open-Minded.* The best leaders are the ones whose minds are never closed, who are interested in hearing new points of view, and who are eager to deal with new issues. Even after decisions have been made, a leader should be willing to listen to contrary views and new approaches. Leaders shouldn't change their minds too frequently after a major decision has been made, but if they never reconsider, they are beginning to show a degree of rigidity and inflexibility that can spell trouble for the organization.

19. *Leaders Should Establish and Maintain High Standards of Dignity.* When standards of dignity are established and emphasized, everyone can take pride in both the accomplishments and the style of the operation. The leader's role is multifaceted. By dressing well, being well mannered, avoiding profanity, helping subordinates through personal or family crises, conducting ceremonies with dignity, welcoming newcomers with warmly written personal letters, leaders can accomplish a great deal. A

happy combination of substance and style leads to high performance and morale.

20. *Leaders Should Exude Integrity.* Leaders should not only talk about integrity, they must also operate at a high level of integrity. They should emphasize both personal and institutional integrity. They should take corrective action when there are violations of integrity and upgrade the standards of institutional integrity over time. A leader should also ensure that everybody understands the leader's fundamental commitment to the values of their institutions. Soon after taking over a leadership position, a leader should look for ways to demonstrate this commitment to integrity. Institutional integrity cannot lie dormant until a crisis occurs; integrity must be ingrained and must be supported by the leader and the organizational community. Of all the qualities a leader must have, integrity is the most important.

2/TAKING OVER:
the vital nature of the transition

MANY INDIVIDUALS taking over leadership positions fail to think through the transition process. They fail to plan to take charge, and so fail to maximize their opportunities to be well prepared for their new leadership responsibilities. By approaching the transition process in a systematic way and following a checklist carefully, a leader can be much more effective in the first few important weeks after taking over. The transition process is particularly important for someone coming into a large or complex organization.

One of the first things a new leader might do is to ask the present leader to make a tape recording outlining major issues, concerns, problems and frustrations that have occurred in the organization. On this tape, the departing leader should also discuss the personalities within the organization with considerable emphasis on immediate subordinates; a frank evaluation of the major personnel problems that exist, and a candid analysis of people who need counselling and people who probably should be re-assigned should be included. Additionally, the incumbent should outline in that tape any "skeletons in the closet" that exist in the organization so that the new leader can be sensitive to issues and problems which might not be visible during the crucial first few months. A caution here is in order: some new leaders prefer not to get an evaluation from the departing leader on the various strengths and weaknesses of subordinates in order to give subordinates a clean slate. I disagree with this approach because some major mistakes can be made by a new leader that can do great harm to an organization if the game is played with a partial deck of cards with regard to a new leader's knowledge of the strengths and weaknesses of key personnel.

If possible, the new leader should be permitted to have a few weeks before assuming new responsibilities to ask a number of transition questions. These questions should be answered (preferably in writing but, if not, orally) by the present leader, by the deputy, or by some key individuals within the organization. The most important questions to ask are: What is the mission, role, or desired output of the organization? What is the strategic plan? Financial situation? Debt to equity ratio? What goals have been established? And what are the established priorities? What is the current state of morale? Here it would be advisable to review the organization's most recent evaluation report to see what steps have been taken to correct deficiencies.

It is very common for organizations to lose sight of the desired output as leaders get caught up in solving day-to-day problems; yet, the output (or mission) must remain the first and foremost concern of the leader. There are a variety of other questions which the new leader should ask before taking over the job; many of these are outlined in the transition checklist in Appendix A.

What are the various means of communication that you have available to interact creatively with your subordinates? In many large organizations there are newspapers or newsletters published on a regular basis that will give you the opportunity to write a column outlining a subject that you want to share with your subordinates. Local radio or television is a marvelous way to reach the members of your team and their families. Staff meetings, trips to subordinate organizations, and speeches to various groups are just a few of the ways an active leader can reach out and communicate.

Who will report directly to you and how large is your span of control? A careful reading of the personnel records ahead of time as well as discussions with your predecessor and your superior can help you assess their qualifications. The personnel or human resources officer in a large organization will be an important source of information.

What constituencies will you be serving either directly or indirectly? Leaders of large organizations normally have to serve many constituencies, including their subordinates and their families, the retired community, interest groups, reserve organizations, alumni, etc. It is useful to find out whom to meet with and who best represents the interests of these constituencies.

Who is your immediate boss and what are his/her leadership and management styles? Before taking charge, you should meet with your boss and get an evaluation of your new job as well as an understanding of your superior's satisfactions and dissatisfactions with the organization you are about to lead. You should also meet with the key staff agency heads who work for your boss to get their views of problem areas and strengths within your new organization.

Are you responsible for geographically separated organizations? Do they report directly or indirectly to you? Most large organizations have geographically separated plants, divisions or units that report to the top leader either directly or indirectly. It is easy for the leader to get caught up in a combination of corporate business at headquarters and in various outreach responsibilities, neglecting field operations. A general rule to follow is to spend a disproportionate amount of time with field organizations to demonstrate your concern, interest, and respect, as well as to update these organizations on your concerns and your changes in policy and plans.

What is the standard of integrity in the organization? Without constant nurturing, high standards of ethics can rapidly deteriorate as one breach of institutional standards quickly leads to another. The leader should review the reporting and inspection systems to ensure that they reinforce rather than undermine integrity.

What are the various standards of discipline? It is reasonably easy to ascertain whether deadlines are being met, if the products being produced are of high quality, and if overall performance is meeting acceptable standards. The leader should look carefully at the performance record of subordinate organizations and staff agencies to ensure that standards are being met and, when they are not, that prompt, appropriate action is taken.

What documents should you read and in what order? Plans, policy statements, and organizational histories (if available) are fine places to start your reading program. Your deputy or executive vice president should help prepare this list of documents for you. He or she should prioritize these documents so you can read the most important ones first.

Is there anything that, if made public, could embarrass my predecessor, the organization, or me? In other words, are there "skeletons" and, if so, in what closet? It is important to ascertain if there are key individuals in the organization who have serious health problems, including alcoholism, drug abuse and psychiatric difficulties. In addition, it is useful to root out institutional "skeletons in the closet" which may not have been revealed in normal reporting for fear that the organization or the boss will look bad, or that corporate profits will suffer.

What is the overall size of the organization you are about to lead? Is the present organizational structure effective and is it, at the same time, encouraging initiative and innovation? The new leader needs to dig into issues of organizational effectiveness to ensure that there is a workable span of control without too many people reporting directly to the leader.

It also is useful to find out if subordinate leaders have regular counselling sessions with their subordinates, and if poor performance is being identified and corrected. Additionally, the leader should look at the continuity of the organization for the next few years so that scheduled retirements and other departures of key subordinates can be identified and replacements recruited well in advance of departure dates. In addition, younger officials will look to you to establish a promotion system that will give them opportunities for upward mobility.

It is always useful to take an objective look at the individual that you are replacing. If the organization is in great shape and your predecessor has been a popular leader, it may be worthwhile to continue past policies, to let everybody know that you are honored to follow someone of such stature, and to articulate your hope that you will be able to keep the unit performance and morale at its high level. If the individual is very popular, but the performance of the organization has been fairly low, you have a greater challenge. You must be willing to demand higher performance levels without denigrating the leader you have just replaced. If you are following an individual who is very cold, harsh, or unpopular, but the organization has been performing well, then your task is easy. By reaching out to people, by thanking and complimenting them often, and by being approachable, you can lift performance even higher by enhancing morale. Finally, if you take over an organization that is performing badly you can take the approach that it is time for everyone in the organization to chart a new course, to recognize the deficiencies of past performance and to work together to upgrade performance levels across the entire organization.

Two common problems with decisionmaking should be discussed with subordinates during the initial phases of the transition process: the "Oh, by the way" problem and the "nonconcurrence through silence" issue. By discussing these issues with your key staff officials and your subordinate leaders, you can help them understand some important ground rules with regard to the decisionmaking process under your leadership.

The "Oh, by the way" problem is a common phenomenon in most large organizations. At the end of a scheduled meeting, the leader will sometimes be approached by a subordinate who will say, "Oh, by the way, I would like to raise a new issue and get your decision." Immediately, you should be cautious, since often the issue requires coordination, and a quick decision by you can be a mistake. A useful way to handle this situation is to listen carefully, to ask the individual to coordinate the issue with other staff and field agencies, and to decline the opportunity to make a decision (or even a tentative decision) prior to the completion of the coordination process. Sometimes this requires extraordinary self-discipline on the part of the leader since the subordinate may be pushing hard for a quick decision— there may be some urgency involved—and the leader may not want to appear indecisive. However, in many cases, a quick decision is a bad idea and will come back to haunt the leader.

Leaders may wish to establish a "no nonconcurrence through silence" rule. Subordinates who do not concur with the decisions being made in meetings and discussions must understand that they have a responsibility to speak up. By remaining silent during these discussions, they do the leader a grave disservice. A major part of subordinates' duties is to speak out on issues, particularly when they disagree with either the context or the thrust of the discussion in which a decision is being made. The leader must create a decisionmaking environment in which subordinates feel free to express concerns, raise new options, and disagree with the leader and others. Leaders must work hard to avoid "groupthink" in which there is too much compatibility and a consensus on issues is arrived at too quickly. False consensus, excessive conformity, and group-think are not in the interest of any large organization. Even though the concerns raised by subordinates may be parochial or ill-considered, the leader must be willing to listen carefully to these concerns before a final decision is made. There is a direct relationship between the thoroughness and openness of the decisionmaking process and the effectiveness of the implementation process. If subordinates are given a full opportunity to express their views prior to the making of the decision, they will be more willing to carry out the decision after it is made, even though the decision may not be the one that the subordinate would have chosen.

Leaders who have gone through the transition process carefully and systematically and know what they want to do, when they want to do it, how they want to make decisions, and how they want to approach issues, can quickly get the attention and respect of their people and can make a big difference in both the future performance and self-esteem of the unit. If the new leader also creates an atmosphere that encourages high integrity, planning, and creativity, the organization can soon become the model for others to emulate.

Having addressed all these questions, the new leader should assess the performance of the organization and its ability to accomplish its mission. Higher headquarters staff and your immediate superior can be very helpful, and considerable time should be spent reading the reports of and talking to auditors, inspectors and evaluators. It is quite common to find an organization having an inflated view of its own level of performance. Although more unusual, there are organizations which, at times, have a deflated view of themselves; therefore, it is important for the new leader to walk into this job with an objective understanding of both the perceptions and the realities. Thorough assessment is vital. By establishing goals early and articulating those goals in a way that can be easily understood by subordinates, a leader can quickly establish agendas, priorities and objectives. For the conscientious leader, this process never ends.

3/ESTABLISHING STANDARDS:
personal and institutional integrity

UPON ASSUMPTION OF the leadership of an organization, it is important for the leader to make clear the standards of integrity that are to be adhered to by the organization. One way to do that is through the company, post, or base newspaper or a newsletter where the leader can write down precisely what is meant by integrity and what standards are to be established and maintained. The new leader should also talk about integrity in shop get-togethers, in staff meetings, with subordinate leaders, at commander's calls, and so forth. In the process of writing and talking about integrity, the leader should use examples from personal experience.

Early in your tenure as the leader you should look for opportunities to demonstrate, within the context of the organization which you now lead, your commitment to integrity. Perhaps a brief personal example will best illustrate this point. At Bitburg, Germany, we were conducting a NATO exercise and my intelligence officer got up in front of all the pilots to outline the reporting guidelines. He said he wanted the pilots to report that they had expended four missiles and half of the rounds from the gatling gun and state that each pilot had shot down four enemy aircraft. I interrupted the intelligence officer because of my concern about these ground rules. I said to the assembled group: "We will not do that; I don't want to set an example, even in an exercise, of dishonest reporting. What I want you to do is go up, intercept the inbound aggressor airplanes, make your simulated attacks and report what you actually accomplish. If you shoot down four airplanes in simulated combat, report four airplanes. If you shoot down no airplanes, report no airplanes. Don't falsify reports just to exercise the system." It was a fine opportunity to demonstrate that we would not set a pattern of prevarication in our day-to-day activities, but that we would report honestly and fairly what we did.

Another true story also illustrates my point about personal integrity. Babe Didrikson-Zaharias was a great athlete in the 1932 Olympics and later became a professional golfer. While playing in a tournament on the golf tour she noticed she had somehow played the wrong ball. When the round was over she penalized herself two strokes which cost her first place in the tournament. Later, in a quiet conversation, one of her friends asked her, "Babe, why did you do that? No one would have known that you used the wrong ball." Babe answered, "I would have known." It is this kind of personal integrity we need to emphasize in all institutions and organizations in our country—a personal commitment to integrity that is deep and profound. In combination with a strong commitment to institutional or corporate integrity, this personal strength of character is what leaders should stress and stress frequently. There are people who would never lie in their personal lives but who would lie for their institution. Yet institutional integrity is just as important and, in the national security arena, more important than personal integrity, although they are inseparable. Low levels of institutional integrity damage the credibility of the organization, your own credibility, personal trust, and mutual respect.

Another aspect of integrity which leaders should consider is "protecting their signature." Since most of the letters, memoranda, staff papers, messages, regulations, and directives that they sign will be prepared by members of their staff, they should do an "integrity check" before they sign the paper. From my experience the most common violation of integrity is in the personnel system. The general who states that "this is the best lieutenant colonel working for me" can only do this about once a year, or he undermines his credibility within the personnel and promotion system. There is a great irony in this area. By pushing too many people too hard, the leader hurts them all because his signature and his endorsement lose value and, in fact, sometimes become a negative factor which hurts his people.

An example of a problem with institutional integrity also may help to illustrate this point. In the early 1980s, a Chief of Staff of one of the military services received a briefing from his staff on the "Program" for the next five years. This Program outlined the staff's collective advice on how funds should be allocated yearly for the upcoming five-year period. When the briefing was completed, the Chief of Staff said quietly but firmly: "This is a dishonest Program; I will not submit it in its present form to the Secretary of Defense." The staff had developed the Program in a way that tried to maximize opportunities to get as much as possible of what that Service needed. What was ignored or was, at least, circumvented, were some of the high priorities of the President and the Secretary of Defense. The staff was "gaming" the Program, and the Chief of Staff, being faithful to the letter and the spirit of the guidance he had received from the Secretary of Defense, was unwilling to sign the document.

Many issues of integrity in the highly politicized atmosphere of Washington are complex and fuzzy, but too often people take the manipulative road and integrity suffers. All leaders in government should remind themselves periodically of Grover Cleveland's candid comment, "Public office is a public trust." George Washington perhaps said it best when he advised, "Labor to keep alive in your breast that little spark of celestial fire called conscience."

4/HIRING:
the right people for the right jobs

ONE OF THE MORE important responsibilities for a leader of a large organization is hiring immediate subordinates and other key people in the organization. Personnel records and resumés are useful starting points in identifying those individuals who are clearly strong candidates for the position under consideration. However, additional research needs to be done through contacts with individuals who know the prospective candidate. It is particularly useful to talk to people who have been the individual's bosses in recent years to get candid evaluations of the performance of the individual in other job situations. All this research is well worth doing to ensure the selection process is complete and is as objective as possible. However, in many cases, this research is not enough and an interview is necessary.

The interview should be conducted systematically; a checklist should be used (although the checklist should be in the leader's head rather than on paper, in order to increase the informality of the interview process), and key questions should be asked. See Appendix A.

The first question asked of a prospective key subordinate should be: *"Do you want the job and why?"* If the candidate is not really interested in the job, has serious reservations about the job, or has motivations for the job you don't find useful or particularly attractive, the interview can be wrapped up quickly, and the individual eliminated from consideration. In the following discussion, there are a number of additional questions. These can be asked in any order.

Why should I hire you? What are your strengths and what are your weaknesses? These questions sometimes set an interviewee back a bit, but it is very useful to find out how introspective the individual is. If the individual lists a large number of strengths and no weaknesses or vice versa, you may have identified an individual who will not serve you well. An individual who not only outlines individual strengths but is aware of, and working on, weaknesses is an individual who probably deserves very serious consideration. Those people who are too self-assured to the point of arrogance or lack self-confidence are not likely to be major contributors to your organization.

What are the best books that you have read in recent years; why do you consider them so good; what insights did these books give you? This is a good way to find out how well-read an individual is—how intellectually curious, how open to ideas, suggestions, and insights that good books can provide, and how well this person is keeping up with his/her discipline or profession. It has been my experience that people who are not widely read and who do not have the intellectual curiosity or the interest to read professional journals and books that help them improve are basically self-limited. They are not likely to grow and to make major contributions beyond the level of their present competence. If you find a person who is well-read, you can probably gain some interesting and useful insights about the individual and you can have a discussion which will be a learning experience on both sides. The best leaders often are the ones who are intellectually curious.

What is your leadership philosophy and style? This is a good way to ascertain whether the individual knows how to operate efficiently, knows what subordinates feel, knows how to set goals and priorities and knows how to be introspective. Another question that is useful is, "If I were to ask your present subordinates how they would describe your leadership style, what would they say?" The answer can be insightful because it can quickly draw out the attitude that the individual has toward subordinates and whether the individual is willing to acknowledge the fact that there may be some subordinates who are uncomfortable with his/her personal style. The answer, in combination with what you might find out from other sources, can give you an understanding of how well this individual grasps the realities of the present situation.

If you are not selected for this position, who would you recommend? This is a useful question to find out how a person judges the job, the qualities that are needed for it, and how closely the applicant is in contact with other individuals with similar qualifications. It also will bring out how willing an individual is to acknowledge that there may be others who are as well, or better, qualified for this job.

Are there any "skeletons in your closet"? This is a sensitive question and is best asked in a more considerate way, such as, "Are there any general health, family, psychiatric, or other problems that are worrying you that may cause you difficulties or prevent your full effectiveness in this job?" or "Is there anything that would be helpful for me to know now which might be an embarrassment if it surfaces later?" In any case, such a question needs to be asked to help determine how candid the individual is willing to be with you. You may want to hire the person regardless of his or her response, but it's useful to have all the cards on the table. Such questions tend to surface those cards. If, in fact, important information is withheld from you that you find out from other sources, you will discover that this person is unwilling to be honest and candid.

What are your long-term personal goals? It's helpful to find out where an individual is heading in life. Does this person want to work for you forever or just want this job for a year or two? What are his/her goals after this? Is the applicant hyperambitious or ambitious in a positive way?

If you were in charge of this organization what would you do? This is a way to find out if the candidate has original ideas and insights, and whether there is a willingness to speak up about aspects of the organization that the individual doesn't like or which make him/her uncomfortable. If, for instance, the candidate says nothing, you might want to ask yourself, does this person have the ability to make significant changes where needed, or is this someone who will always be satisfied with the status quo?

What is it that annoys you in your present organization? This is a question that you could ask someone who already works for you. It is also a useful question to ask individuals who do not yet work for you regarding another organization. You might be able to learn a great deal about their personalities. Aspects about their interaction in an organizational framework might be revealed that may reinforce your desire to hire them, or, conversely, give you indications that you would not be comfortable with them.

What are the standards of integrity in your present organization? This is a good way to lead into the integrity question. Do prospective employees have high standards of personal integrity? Do they set high standards of institutional integrity? Do they think or care much about integrity? This can lead to a useful discussion on the issues of institutional and personal ethics and the role that they play in an organizational framework.

Who in your present organization do you respect the most and why? This question tends to highlight certain aspects of personality and background that may provide insights into what a candidate thinks are the important aspects of leadership. If a person admires a strong leader and knows why, as well as what leadership qualities he/she would like to emulate, you may have discovered an individual who has been seriously thinking about leadership and who may be the kind of person you would want to hire as one of your subordinate leaders.

What is the toughest problem you have faced in your career? How did you handle it? This question can be a useful way to determine how well the individual has been tested and what has been learned from a tough experience. It is one way to determine how introspective an individual is.

Since the hiring process is important, it should not be delegated except in certain situations. If you, as the boss, have a trusted deputy who has great insights into the personalities of individuals, has had a lot of experience in interviewing people for jobs, has a good feeling for the organization and knows your particular desires and proclivities, delegating the hiring practice to your deputy makes good sense. It's also sometimes useful to draw together a search committee that may have expertise that you don't have and whose members would be capable of asking the most relevant questions. You can use this committee to screen out and reduce the list to a small number; but, ultimately, the leader must make the choice.

A leader should be actively involved in hiring those individuals who work directly for him. Subordinate leaders should normally be given the authority to hire their subordinates. If a big leader wishes to maintain veto authority over the hiring of key subordinates who will not work directly for him/her, this veto should be used with great care. The veto can help reduce cronyism on the part of subordinate leaders, but it should actually be used very seldom.

Finally, leaders should fully consider the subtle but important aspect of leader-subordinate relationships known commonly as "chemistry" when evaluating various candidates for a key position. The leader should consider the chemistry factor not only in subordinate-leader interactions but also in peer relationships among subordinates. This is one of the reasons that interviews are important; a set of personnel records cannot help very much in determining how well an individual will fit into the environment you have established in your organization.

5/COUNSELLING
SUBORDINATES:
the value of one-on-ones

A LEADER OF AN organization should have private sessions with immediate subordinates about once every six months to deal specifically with performance counselling. The purpose of these sessions is to trade ideas, insights and suggestions, and to learn about the health of the organization. It is an opportunity for personal counselling but, to an even greater extent, it is an opportunity for subordinates to talk quietly, off the record, with the boss in a meaningful way, to get things off their chests, and to suggest ideas and initiatives. Further, individual objectives for improvement can be set for review six months later. These sessions also give subordinates the feeling that their ideas really count and that the boss is interested in listening to them.

In observing leaders from many nations at various levels, it has been my experience that these one-on-one sessions are the exception rather than the rule. Although leaders talk about how they counsel their people, in actuality counselling sessions seldom take place. A quick meeting in the hall, a brief comment or two in a staff meeting, or a passing comment here and there are not counselling sessions.

A useful way to cover the important issues in a counselling session is to ask the following questions:

What aspects of this organization do you like the most? It is useful to start the session on a positive note. This question can be a useful "ice-breaker" since the subordinate may be a bit uncomfortable in the first few minutes in the front office with the boss.

What areas around here bother you the most? This question allows the subordinate to voice those areas of real heartburn. It might be that the subordinate does not like the job, the secretary, the work hours, the level of authority, the living conditions, the pay, or the amount of recognition received. It is a good opportunity to "smoke out" those things that really bother subordinates.

What are your ideas for improving this organization? This is an opportunity not only to get some ideas but also to find out where the "idea people" are. In every organization there are only a few people who actually have innovative ideas. This question often helps identify the folks who really care about improving the organization and have ideas about how to do so.

What policies, procedures, tactics, subordinate organizations, systems, etc., should we divest ourselves of and on what kind of a schedule (now, next year, five years from now, etc.)? Here's a way to discover whether the individual has thought about the problem of what programs we ought to abandon, what things we are doing that inhibit mission accomplishment, what things were useful to do in the past but are no longer useful, and what kind of divestiture strategy we should develop.

In your judgment, who are the most innovative, helpful and cooperative people in this organization? "Who are the people who are not pulling their load?" is often an unfair question and one that people are reluctant to answer. If you ask them, "Who are the best people?" you'll not only find out who the best people are, but you'll also notice, over time, who is seldom or never mentioned. The ones who are never mentioned are normally the ones not pulling their load, not being cooperative, or who have some other problem. In most cases, you will know who the best people are already but, on occasion, you will be surprised. Someone who is particularly quiet, for instance, might be mentioned as an absolutely marvelous and contributing individual.

What are your personal goals while you are in this organization? This is a fine way to ascertain the goals, dreams, and aspirations of your subordinates. Some will prefer to stay at their present levels; others will want to move to another division or location; others will want to move upward. Answers to this question can be very helpful as the leader does personnel planning. Where and to what job would you like to go next, why and when? Here you get an idea of an employee's long-range plans: Where would you like to go next? When would you like to go? What ambitions do you have? How happy are you here? Many insights about your people and organization surface as a result of these questions.

What do you consider to be your most significant weaknesses? Again, if the individual doesn't think any weaknesses exist, you may have a problem right there. In many cases, the individual may outline personal weaknesses fairly well, but may miss one or two areas. This gives you the opportunity to probe gently about a person's ability to write, to speak, to cooperate, to lead, to manage. You can also probe into other areas of possible weakness that may not have been identified. Although a delicate question, it often opens the door to excellent counselling opportunities.

What self-improvement programs do you have underway? Are you pursuing advanced education? Are you taking professional courses? Are you in a Toastmaster's Club to learn how to be a better speaker? Are you taking speed reading courses? If the individual is doing nothing for self-improvement, you have an opportunity to highlight the value of self-improvement.

What do you think your chances are for promotion to the next level, and in what time frame? Here you get an opportunity to have individuals evaluate their own potential for promotion and for moving up to higher levels of responsibility. You will find out whether their expectations are inflated, as they are in some cases. If they do have inflated expectations and you are aware of weak or mediocre professional records, you can give them a candid appraisal. It is important that you be frank as well as factual so that individuals with poor performance records are not destroyed emotionally if they fail to be promoted at some later date.

What bothers you the most about my decisions and my leadership style? In what areas have my decisions or policies caused you to waste your time? Here's a great opportunity to find out a little bit about yourself. Answers to that question may include: "You're too intense;" "You're too hard on people;" "You've put too much emphasis in certain areas and not enough in others;" "What we are doing in a certain area is a waste of time and money." Some people, of course, will tell you that you're wonderful and not give you any indication of your problem areas, but the better, more mature subordinates will almost always say "Yes, there are a few areas; let me make a few suggestions."

What are the goals that you have established for your organization? Here you are asking subordinates what goals they have set for their own organizations. Do their goals conform to the goals you have established for the parent organization? Perhaps the individual has established goals that are more thoughtful or innovative than your own.

Please evaluate the performance of the organization, unit, or group that you led over the past six months. Please outline the high and low points of the period. This is a useful way to ascertain the objectivity of subordinate leaders when it comes to their own organizations.

The counselling checklist should not be read; it should be in your head. At the end of the counselling session, you have the responsibility not only to point out the strengths of the individual, but also to point out weaknesses. If you call in persons who are not doing particularly well and do not tell them so, you are not conducting honest, fair, and complete counselling sessions. Counselling takes a lot of time and is hard work; sometimes the reaction to criticism on the part of the subordinate becomes very emotional, but it is something that needs to be scheduled regularly and done well. For each one-on-one session, you should allow one hour. Often the session may last only 20 or 30 minutes, but there may be a requirement to listen for a long time when serious problems surface. As a general guide, the session should start and end on positive notes. Even if the individual has not been performing well, a compliment at the end of the session is important.

Sometimes, your counselling session with a subordinate must concentrate wholly on his or her shortcomings or failures. These sessions are easy to avoid or postpone, but they must be done in a timely and tactful manner. If a subordinate makes a serious mistake that clearly requires corrective action, you should immediately have a private meeting. Public admonishment should be avoided, but private counselling should take place quickly and firmly and all important areas should be covered carefully and systematically. An excellent example of counselling of this type was Robert E. Lee's session with J.E.B. Stuart when he arrived at the Gettysburg battlefield two days late. The following comes from

Michael Shaara's Pulitzer Prize-winning historical novel, *The Killer Angels*.*

> He saw a man coming toward him, easy gait, rolling and serene, instantly recognizable: Jeb Stuart. Lee stood up. This must be done. Stuart came up, saluted pleasantly, took off the plumed hat and bowed.
>
> 'You wish to see me, sir?'
>
> 'I asked to see you alone,' Lee said quietly. 'I wished to speak with you alone, away from other officers. That has not been possible until now. I am sorry to keep you up so late.'
>
> 'Sir, I was not asleep,' Stuart drawled, smiled, gave the sunny impression that sleep held no importance, none at all.
>
> Lee thought: here's one with faith in himself. Must protect that. And yet, there's a lesson to be learned. He said, 'Are you aware, General, that there are officers on my staff who have requested your court-martial?'
>
> Stuart froze. His mouth hung open. He shook his head once quickly, then cocked it to one side.
>
> Lee said, 'I have not concurred. But it is the opinion of some excellent officers that you have let us all down.'
>
> 'General Lee,' Stuart was struggling. Lee thought: now there will be anger. 'Sir,' Stuart said tightly, 'if you will tell me who these gentlemen . . . '

---

*From *The Killer Angels* by Michael Shaara. Copyright© 1974 by Michael Shaara. Reprinted by permission of David McKay Co., a Division of Random House, Inc.

'There will be none of that.' Lee's voice was cold and sharp. He spoke as you speak to a child, a small child, from a great height. 'There is no time for that.'

'I only ask that I be allowed—'

Lee cut him off. 'There is no time,' Lee said. He was not a man to speak this way to a brother officer, a fellow Virginian; he shocked Stuart to silence with the iciness of his voice. Stuart stood like a beggar, his hat in his hands.

'General Stuart,' Lee said slowly, 'you were the eyes of this army.' He paused.

Stuart said softly, a pathetic voice, 'General Lee, if you please . . .' But Lee went on.

'You were my eyes. Your mission was to screen this army from the enemy cavalry and to report any movement by the enemy's main body. That mission was not fulfilled.'

Stuart stood motionless.

Lee said, 'You left this army without word of your movements, or of the movements of the enemy, for several days. We were forced into battle without adequate knowledge of the enemy's position, or strength, without knowledge of the ground. It is only by God's grace that we have escaped disaster.'

'General Lee.' Stuart was in pain, and the old man felt pity, but this was necessary; it had to be done as a bad tooth has to be pulled, and there was no turning away. Yet even now he felt the pity rise, and he wanted to say, it's all right, boy, it's all right; this is only a lesson, just one painful quick moment of learning, over in a moment, hold on, it'll be all right. His voice began to soften. He could not help it.

'It is possible that you misunderstood my orders. It is possible I did not make myself clear. Yet this must be clear; you with your cavalry are the eyes of the army. Without your cavalry, we are blind, and that has happened once, but must never happen again.'

There was a moment of silence. It was done. Lee wanted to reassure him, but he waited, giving it time to sink in, to take effect, like medicine. Stuart stood breathing audibly. After a moment he reached down and unbuckled his sword, theatrically, and handed it over with high drama in his face. Lee grimaced, annoyed, put his hands behind his back, half turned his face. Stuart was saying that since he no longer held the General's trust, but Lee interrupted with acid vigor.

'I have told you that there is no time for that. There is a fight tomorrow, and we need you. We need every man, God knows. You must take what I have told you and learn from it as a man does. There has been a mistake. It will not happen again. I know your quality. You are a good soldier. You are as good a cavalry officer as I have known, and your service to this army has been invaluable. I have learned to rely on your information; all your reports are always accurate. But no report is useful if it does not reach us. And that is what I wanted you to know. Now.' He lifted a hand. 'Let us talk no more of this.'

6/FIRING:
the role of the leader

LEADERS OF ORGANIZA-
tions occasionally need to remove people for a number of reasons: to remove incompetents, to reinforce
standards, to punish violations of integrity, etc. The
leader normally should fire individuals himself and
not delegate that task to a lower level official. If,
however, a leader has a very large organization
some delegation may be necessary. In any case, people who work directly for the leader should be fired
by the boss.

Before an individual is removed for any reason,
it is the responsibility of the leader to call the individual in for counselling, to explain forthrightly the
deficiency, and to let the individual know where his
job performance has been substandard. If, after a
period of a few months, the performance standards
still do not reach an acceptable level, the leader
should again see the individual privately and with

firmness relieve him of his position. One approach is to tell the individual that the leader has lost confidence in the employee's ability to do that job. During this session it is important for the leader to give the individual who is being removed the opportunity to explain what problems exist and how he feels about this action; the leader should be a patient and passive listener. It is a very traumatic experience for an individual to be fired, for in most cases it will be the first time. The leader has a responsibility to help the employee work through this difficult experience. Let the employee know specifically that you're asking him to leave because you feel that it's your responsibility as a leader. It is also useful during this session to point out that now, in being removed, the employee might go through a difficult period in life, both personally, and with the family. You should talk at length to the individual about future prospects. If appropriate, offer to help in finding the employee a new position. You should explain that you will write a final effectiveness report or evaluation with care to ensure that the individual's strengths as well as weaknesses are outlined fairly.

There may be some cases in which the individual has failed so badly in performance, integrity, or some other area, that you must be quite tough on the final report. If the employee is being fired for cause, there should be no question remaining about why he is being fired and that the cause is an important one.

People often get fired because they are not doing a particular job well, but they still have talents and abilities that can be applied elsewhere. It is often your responsibility as a leader to ensure that such individuals are moved into positions where they will have the opportunity to utilize and exploit their talents.

In some cases it's appropriate for the leader to suggest early retirement or a very significant job change. If the individual has demonstrated a real weakness in personal ability to do very basic things within the organization, it is useful to be straightforward with the individual and suggest that retirement might be in order.

It might be helpful here to explain a few situations I have faced in having to remove individuals for specific reasons. While Commandant of the National War College, I had to remove a professor before the end of the academic year because I was getting bad feedback on his attitude, his teaching ability, and his failure to organize his courses properly. I called him in and told him it was time for him to move on and explained why. We were able to find him a job where he was clearly competent. Although he was bitter about his experiences at the College and was not pleased with me, I think the move was best for him, and certainly best for the College. If he had stayed at the College, there probably would have been further damage to his career as a result of his continuing failure to meet our expectations.

Another example occurred when I was the Chief Planner for the Air Force and had to remove a colonel who was in charge of a division because of his authoritarian approach to leadership. He was very hard on his people. He treated a group of very talented majors and lieutenant colonels as if they were unreliable or immature or both. He moved on to another job which took advantage of his creativity and energy, but had no one to supervise directly. He performed superbly.

A third example occurred when I removed an Air Force colonel who was a base commander. He was in charge of about 800 individuals, including civil engineers, security police and many other people responsible for the combat support of a tactical fighter wing in Europe. This man was married and lived with his wife on base; he also had a girl friend downtown. He was embarrassing himself, his family, and the Wing since it was widely known that his girl friend had moved into a nearby apartment. I told him that I could not tolerate that kind of activity, especially in light of strictly established policies which he, himself, was responsible for enforcing.

Another example of note would be the alcoholic major who worked for me when I was at an international headquarters. He was from a European nation. After some counselling by me and the senior officer from his country, I asked him to leave short of his normal tour of duty. It took a number of months before we could move him out because of the personnel system in his country. He was removed for chronic absenteeism and his unwillingness to face up to his problem and seek professional help.

There are a number of subtleties to be considered when the leader makes the decision to remove a subordinate from a position. There is a continuum of choices between a "hard" firing and a "soft" firing, and the leader should think through the various options quite carefully. Leaders should seek advice from their deputies, their lawyers, and their personnel officers (and, on occasion, from their expert on public relations, their psychiatrist, their chaplain). Before the individual who is to be removed from office is called in, the leader must fully understand what authority is available, what the legal implications may be, how easy it will be to find a suitable replacement, etc. Consideration of the impact on the performance and morale of the organization which may result from this action may also be in order.

Leaders who never fire anyone may be doing a disservice to their institution; as a result, many other people take advantage of the fact that they are safe from the real discipline of being removed from office. Therefore, a deserved firing is not only the right thing to do, but it also sets the tone to let people know that there are certain standards of performance and ethics to be met. It is an important part of any leader's responsibility to fire individuals who, *after proper counselling,* fail to live up to these standards.

7/LEADING IN CRISES:
coolness and flexibility

NO MATTER HOW WELL A leader plans, anticipates problems, and reacts in normal day-to-day activity, crises will occur. The enormity of a crisis, the time constraints, the fact that people's lives may be in danger, or other unique factors will present challenges that will test a leader severely and often call upon skills and leadership techniques not normally tested.

A major aspect of crisis leadership is the requirement for flexibility and innovation. The leader must be willing to show flexibility, be open to suggestions on how to solve crises, and be willing to allow emergent leaders to come forward to assist. A hallmark of crisis leadership is keeping things simple—asking people to do things that they are already trained to do, and not asking them to do new things with which they are unfamiliar.

In many crises, the leader may not have the communications on hand to be able to manage them. Additionally, the leader may be isolated from the crisis (e.g., is a hostage), be hurt or injured, have had a heart attack, or for other reasons been incapacitated. In anticipation of facing crises, the leader must identify and train other leaders who can pick up the ball and handle the situation.

The training aspect of crisis management is very similar to the training aspect of combat leadership. It should be set up in such a way that the real stresses with which one might be expected to deal are simulated with the greatest possible accuracy. Therefore, if you are going to run a crisis exercise, you would want to put the individuals in the actual situations and locations where they would expect to deal with the crisis, whether it be a command post, the front office, or a field location. The management of a crisis can be long, drawn out, and full of tension. The inputs in the training exercise should be many; they should be complex and all the information that the individual might need should not be provided. Crisis exercises should have shifts of twelve hours or more so that the individual has to deal with being overburdened and tired. The simulation of wounds, death, and health problems, and the simulated failure of someone to make it to a particular meeting or activity, are important. Simulations which allow emergent leaders to come forward and take over are valuable.

The individual who is involved in handling a crisis must be technically competent and must understand the people, the organization, the mission, the goals, and the priorities. A leader in a peacetime crisis as well as leaders in combat cannot operate with only a superficial knowledge of what the organization is about and what its capabilities are. The leader in a crisis situation also must be dispassionate. The leader must keep an eye on individual performances even while holding the mission as the first priority. Although emotionally involved in the issues, the leader must stand back from the situation and make the choices that ensure that the missions are carried out and the best possible solutions to the problems are achieved. If, in an extreme situation, that means sacrificing the leader's or others' careers, health, or lives for the greater good of the largest number of people, or the greater good of the mission, a true leader must be willing to make that choice or those choices. Such situations often occur in combat.

The parallel between combat leadership and crisis leadership is close, although lives are not always endangered in peacetime crises. Nevertheless, there are the same tensions, the same need for flexibility and innovation, and the same need to keep things basic and simple when tasking individuals and subordinate organizations to carry out responsibilities. The motivational leadership required in combat often is needed in a peacetime crisis to ensure that the individuals work in close harmony. In combat, if soldiers think they have a real chance to succeed, if they trust and respect their leaders, if they have a feeling of individual invulnerability, if they believe the enemy will die, not them, they are more likely to be victorious. Leaders during crises and combat need to operate in a well-trained, yet pragmatic, way; they must not be tied inflexibly to the doctrines of the past that may not apply to fast moving situations of the present.

One of the reasons that it is important for leaders to train sub-leaders and subordinates to carry out important responsibilities is that often in crisis and combat situations numerous leaders are taken out of the game. They are killed, kidnapped, injured, or their health suffers, or they are not in communication with their subordinates. If the subordinate leaders have previously been given the opportunity to grow, be creative, and develop their leadership skills, they are more likely to step forward and exert needed leadership. Such training is critical.

After a crisis is over, it is useful to conduct a "hot wash-up" (a wonderfully descriptive term used throughout the NATO Alliance) which brings together the key people involved in the crisis to analyze what lessons were learned. In addition, an after-action report should be completed with an analysis of points or areas where future crises can be handled better.

One of the most useful techniques for a leader to employ in a crisis is to develop an "opportunity team" or teams, which are not directly involved in the moment-by-moment management of the crisis, but are close enough to the situation to be able to sit back, analyze opportunities, and suggest actions. Because leaders are so busy managing the crisis, they usually have no time to generate ideas on using the crisis to accomplish things that could not be done in non-crisis situations. A small group of innovators, perhaps the corporate long-range planning group, can provide the input of "why don't we try this?" or "have you thought of this option?" This technique can turn a crisis, which is both a challenge and a unique event, into an opportunity for the leader and for the organization.

An excellent example of a leader taking advantage of a crisis was President Kennedy during the Berlin Wall crisis of 1961. He used that crisis as an opportunity to build up conventional forces, to call reserves into active duty, and to deploy units to Europe on short notice for training and deterrent value. He had an "opportunity plan" and he carried it out. Franklin Roosevelt also took advantage of various world crises in the late 1930s and early 1940s to help prepare the United States for war. The initiation of a peacetime draft, lend lease, and the "destroyer deal" are three examples.

Individuals who face a crisis, and combat leaders of the future, should be aware that they will often be short on facts, emotions may be running high, and the "fog of war" will lead to much confusion. Even though all the options may not be ideal, the leader must be decisive. For example, in combat, a leader must somehow order and lead large numbers into battle and send some to their deaths, while, at the same time, tempering courage with wisdom. Leaders of large organizations in combat must exercise a great deal of self-discipline and avoid micromanaging subordinate leaders. Normally, a top combat leader should be dealing with military strategy and operational art and not with tactics or moment-to-moment war-fighting decisions. The top field commanders should spend most of the time planning for the operations of the future—the months and weeks ahead. They should also spend a considerable amount of their time assessing the progress of the war, drawing lessons from successes and failures, and ensuring that these lessons are being incorporated into campaign plans for the future. Too many top leaders, enjoying the luxury of excellent communications, fail to resist the natural temptation to get deeply involved in day-to-day or moment-to-moment decisions. They do their organizations a double disservice by failing to plan and by micromanaging.

From presidents of the United States who pick individual targets to bomb in North Vietnam, to high-level field commanders who love to fly around in helicopters making battalion and company commander-level decisions, the track record of this nation in recent history as far as combat leadership by high-level leaders has been rather poor. Most of the top military leaders in the United States, from now until the end of this century, have observed at first hand the dysfunctional aspects of this micromanagement during the Vietnam War. Hopefully they will avoid these tendencies themselves if and when they are asked to lead large military units into combat.

In the area of combat leadership it is important to remember that war is not a technological problem, it is fundamentally a human problem. Combat leaders must be historically minded, for military and naval history are the laboratories for understanding war.

As the last war recedes into history, it is more and more important for military leaders to study the great theorists of war, the great military leaders of the past, and the great works of military history. Since reading time is always limited, a few particularly insightful books are recommended:

- *On the Psychology of Military Incompetence* by Dixon
- *Generalship, Its Diseases and Their Cures* by Fuller
- *Eisenhower*, Volume I by Ambrose
- The Second and Third Volumes of the *George C. Marshall* biography by Pogue
- *American Caesar* by Manchester
- *Nimitz* by Potter
- The forthcoming analytical histories of Air Force mission areas by the Office of Air Force History
- *The Twenty-Five Year War* by Palmer

When leaders read history they should do so from an analytical framework and they should seek enduring lessons from the historical experiences of others. Leaders in combat, at the strategic, operational, and tactical levels, need more than just experience in war. To paraphrase Plato, experience develops all our great flute players, but also, unfortunately, all our worst flute players. Combat leaders must not only understand and adapt to change, they must also be in control of change. Combat leaders must be comfortable with risk, but must know the difference between risk and gamble. They must shape the enemy while at the same time avoiding being shaped by the enemy. They must know how to reconstitute demoralized units which have gone through psychological collapse.

In peacetime, gaining combat leadership experience is normally impossible and even gaining solid peacetime leadership experience is often difficult. Of the more than 50 United States Army corps commanders in World War II, most of whom were splendid leaders, none had major leadership experience prior to Pearl Harbor. How did so many do so well? One answer may be that they studied war, taught war, debated war, and took their military profession quite seriously. In the days before television, the planning, programming, and budgeting system, the complexities of a multi-alliance structure, and rapid job changes and promotions, military officers had and took the time to study their profession in depth. Clearly, we have Pattons, Nimitzs, MacArthurs, and Eisenhowers in our midst, but unfortunately, they are often too "busy" to think, read, study, and write. This raises an important question for the American military. Can it accomplish its many tasks, provide the leadership for the military services of the Western world, and still find time to prepare itself adequately for the crises and wars of the future? If not, is there a danger that the lack of intellectual and professional preparation for war will weaken the American ability to deter war? It is the responsibility of military leaders to address these questions and to find satisfactory answers to them.

8/DEALING WITH THE DOWN SIDE:
police blotters, failures, and criticism

LEADERS OF LARGE organizations spend considerable time dealing with the unhappy side of human relationships. Problems will surface; it is the responsibility of leaders to ensure that they maintain good feedback loops relating to unfortunate events occurring within their organizations. These feedback loops should be even better than those dealing with more normal and upbeat events. Leaders must actively seek out bad news, but should understand that there will be people at various levels trying to withhold such news from them. The information they do receive often will be just a portion of the total bad news within their organizations.

One useful vehicle for determining what's happening inside an organization is the use of a "police blotter" or similar kind of daily report that might be used by police, security people, lawyers, social action people, chaplains, or mental health counsellors. In the military, as well as in towns and cities, leaders have access to the police blotter. It is a useful instrument to ascertain the morale and discipline of any organization or community. Normally a police blotter is developed on a minute-by-minute basis through a 24-hour period, is collated, and is provided to the leader or commander every morning. It is very useful to have the police blotter on your desk each morning so you can review the events of the previous day. Many of these events are routine; for instance, things like lights left on in certain buildings, doors left unlocked, or minor traffic or parking violations. But in many large organizations, you will also find, almost every day, something of greater concern: a fight in a bar, a demonstration at the front gate, a rape, a child abuse case, a spouse abuse case, a suicide attempt, a bomb threat. The commander should keep track of these activities to ascertain where the specific problems are within organizations and to monitor the corrective action taken by subordinates. The commander should follow up on these events to ensure that justice is served and that the institutional goals established by the leader are being met and followed.

All leaders of large organizations should fully understand that somewhere within their organizations there are often events occurring that have either unethical or illegal aspects. No matter how perceptive and "tuned in" leaders may be, they must realize that there are illegal, unethical or unfortunate activities going on that go unreported. Sexual harassment, racial slurs, petty theft, drug abuse, alcoholism, and such, are the stuff of everyday life in many large organizations. Leaders must ensure that they have the procedures and the institutional support available to identify these problems and solve them as expeditiously as possible.

There should be regular interaction with the lawyer or lawyers who work directly for the leader. Lawyers should be willing, able, and encouraged to be absolutely frank in their discussions with the leader. Decisions need to be made on a regular basis as to whether an accused party needs to be taken to trial, given appropriate administrative punishment, counselled, or fired. On occasion, decisions need to be made about family members and how they can be properly counselled. Advice from your lawyer is similarly helpful concerning activities that someone in the organization is trying to do for the greater good of the organization but which might be illegal or unethical; for example, fund-raising activities such as Bingo games, raffles, slot machines, etc. which are prohibited by state or federal law or, in overseas areas, by local law or status of forces agreements.

The lawyer should be a very important advisor, an individual who has a high level of integrity, is energetic, "tuned in," and a person who believes in maintaining an appropriate balance between the rights of individuals and those individuals' obligations to the organization. Leaders should listen carefully to their lawyers and although, at times, a

65

leader may want to overrule them, this should be done with great care. An individual with substantial legal training and experience can contribute greatly to the leader's thinking and decisionmaking.

When an organization suffers a major setback, the leader should be quick to accept the blame. It is the leader's fault that the organization failed because of poor planning, poor leadership, poor organization or the inability to anticipate potential problems. There is always a temptation to blame subordinates, fate, poor quality of the equipment, lack of guidance from above, or overtasking. The leader should avoid these temptations. To quote the great Alabama football coach, the late Bear Bryant, "There's just three things I ever say. If anything goes bad, then I did it. If anything goes semi-good, then we did it. If anything goes really good, then you did it. That's all it takes to get people to win football games."

Fear of failure is one of the major causes of executive stress. A leader of a large organization should welcome an occasional failure. Failure often demonstrates that the organization is trying new approaches, setting ambitious goals, being innovative and creative and avoiding stand-patism and status-quoism. If leaders of large organizations take their subordinates on an annual off-site retreat, the failures of the past year should be discussed in a very positive way. The leader should compliment the group on the many new approaches taken, identify some of the failures as "heroic failures which taught us all" and those which, at a later time, may turn into grand successes. The leader should help everyone bounce back from failure. By doing so, he can encourage subordinates to continue to reach beyond their grasp in order to accomplish great things.

Soviet military philosophy on leadership raises the important point that the higher the post you occupy, the more strictly you will be judged. A leader is bound to be criticized, both fairly and unfairly, by subordinates within the organization, by his bosses and their staffs, by competitive organizations, and by the press. A leader who becomes very thin-skinned when criticized, or who becomes defensive and somewhat paranoid, is doing a disservice to the organization. By admitting failure early on, the leader of the organization can often put it behind him, take necessary corrective action, and return the organization to a higher level of performance and morale. As a leader, it is important to observe your subordinate leaders and ascertain how well they accept criticism and how willing they are to accept blame for the failures of the organization. The defensive, thin-skinned, "blame-someone-else" individual is unlikely to succeed as a leader of a large organization. It is the mature leader, indeed, who accepts even unfair criticisms with equanimity, calmness and grace.

Those individuals who have reached high leadership positions without one or more major setbacks in their careers are often not well equipped to handle failure and heavy criticism. Therefore, when you are choosing individuals for leadership jobs, you may wish to look into their backgrounds to see if they have met failure and see how well they handled it.

9/COMPLIMENTING CREATIVELY:
saying thank you in many ways

GOOD LEADERS SPEND considerable time complimenting and thanking the people who work for them. It is quite an art to do this in a way that conveys sincerity, compliments people who should be complimented, and subtly leaves out people who do not deserve to be thanked or commended.

Casey Kasem, the radio disc jockey, introduces the Top 40 songs to his listening audience with great enthusiasm. One of the reasons for Kasem's success and popularity is his ability to find *uniqueness* in each song that makes the Top 40. A combination of his creativity, his commitment to research, and his love for his work make many people want to listen to his show.

A few years ago, he made the point that this was the first time in the history of the Top 40 that a

Scottish trio, singing a country-western song, had made it to the Top 10. This introduction triggered a leadership idea. The following week, I made the point to all my subordinate leaders that they should look around at positive things their units had been doing that were unusual or special. By careful research and brainstorming, they were able to find, within our squadron and units, things that were unique or were establishing new standards or setting new records. We were able to highlight these things in the weekly base newspaper with headlines and laudatory stories: "Supply Squadron Establishes Record for Servicing F-15's"; "Security Police Set New Record in Processing of Licenses for Automobiles"; "Fighter Squadron and Maintenance Unit Set New Flying Time (or Sortie) Record," etc. This is a marvelous way to make people feel very special every week; it is a creative way to pay compliments. Many leaders just say, "you all did well," or "I'm proud of you," or "thanks a lot" in redundant ways. Making the "compliment-paying" aspect of your leadership more personal and creative pays dividends in individual and unit morale. The idea of catching people doing things right rather than catching them doing something wrong has universal application.

In most organizations or units, 80 to 90 percent of the people are working very hard to accomplish the mission, to serve the institution, to make the unit look good or to make you look good. People, generally, want to associate with, and participate in, success. It is important to remind yourself that your people are out there working hard and doing a fine job. You should spend a lot of time with these people, complimenting and thanking them. Occasionally when you get people together and praise them, there may be some who do not deserve your praise, but that fact should not deter you from complimenting the group. Individuals not deserving of praise can be dealt with separately and individually. When you thank your people, don't sound angry. Unfortunately, commanders on occasion get up and try to thank their people and it sounds like they are chewing them out. They have not developed the kind of presence that permits them to reach out and figuratively wrap their arms around people to let them know that they respect and appreciate what they are doing. The brilliant, efficient individuals who cannot warmly thank, compliment, and commend their people will always fall well short of their full potential as leaders.

In the area of creative compliments some thought should be given by a leader to developing techniques for complimenting subordinates individually as well as collectively. One of the highest compliments I've ever received was given to me by the late General Jerry O'Malley. He told me that the reason he had chosen me to be the Air Force Planner was because the majors and lieutenant colonels in the Plans Directorate had wanted me. By avoiding the normal rationale and finding a creative way to compliment me, he really touched me. It was as nice a compliment as I could have imagined. It came from a man who had a great understanding of people. Of all the communications skills a leader should develop, praising creatively should be at the top of the list. Leaders should follow the advice of Letitia Baldridge: "Learn how to pay compliments. Start with members of your family, and you will find it will become easier later in life to compliment others. It's a great asset."

A leader must also know how to accept compliments. An excellent guide is to pass every compliment on to your subordinates for, in almost all cases, the success was theirs—their ideas, their efficiency, their hard work, and their creativity—all in marvelous combinations.

An important part of thanking and commending people is knowing their names. In very large organizations it is impossible for the leader to know most of his subordinates' names, but whenever he is about to present awards, compliment an organization publicly, give a speech to a significant number of his subordinates, he should mention a few names of people in the group who are particularly deserving of praise. The leader must do his homework well in this regard and, if possible, meet briefly ahead of time with those individuals he is going to single out publicly. He should ask lots of questions ahead of time such as:

- Has the organization received any outside recognition lately?
- Has anyone in the audience done anything particularly noteworthy lately?
  - —saved someone's life
  - —recovered from major surgery
  - —gotten married
  - —had a baby
  - —returned to work after a long absence

　　—been elected to some important position
- Has the organization recently won a major sports event?
　　—softball tournament
　　—golf match
　　—tennis tournament

If you can, take these individuals out to lunch, hold a seminar with them to get their ideas, or, in general, spend some time with them. During your time with them, call them by their first names. Benefits will rebound throughout the organization.

A leader can "pair" or "bond" with individuals at lower levels in his organization by using these techniques. As these individuals return to their work places they will spread the word that you were approachable, knew their names, showed interest in their ideas. This bonding will lead to greater trust and loyalty throughout the organization. If you know your people's hopes and dreams, if you understand and empathize with their hardships and complaints, you can better thank and compliment them and, just as importantly, you can better plan and make decisions for the good of the organization and the people that you serve.

10/DECENTRALIZING AND GETTING FEEDBACK:
twin dilemmas

THERE IS A GREAT DEAL of discussion in the literature on leadership that pertains to centralization versus decentralization. Most well-run organizations have a balanced amount of centralization and decentralization. At each level, there should be a certain amount of decisionmaking authority and a certain amount of delegation. The best leaders have a solid grasp of all the levels of decision making and authority. They know which decisions should be made at each level and they let the various subordinate leaders know when they feel that decisions are being made at the appropriate level.

It is important for leaders at all levels to get psychic rewards from the work they do, from the authority they have and from the decisions they make. Subordinate leaders should feel responsible

75

and important. With the general trend in America toward better communication and more centralization, all leaders must work deliberately to force decisions down to the appropriate levels.

An example of misplaced authority occurred when the leader of a major military command thought that the captains in the flying squadrons should make all the decisions relating to the flying schedule and the training requirements. He also believed that the lieutenant colonels and colonels should spend a majority of their time ensuring that these captains were properly supported. He was critical of leaders who flew often with the younger officers. The difficulty with this philosophy was that the captains did not have the experience or maturity to make decisions on their own; they needed direction and help from the squadron commanders and wing commanders. The overall result of this approach was a high accident rate, some dangerous training, and the lack of a coherent training program.

Within the context of an organization that has the proper amount of decentralization, leaders must ensure that they have a number of effective feedback mechanisms so that they can be apprised of important events that are going on within their organizations. The normal hierarchical structure (or chain of command in the military) that provides feedback is fine, but other means are needed to supplement it.

An inspection system and an auditing system are methods by which the leader can attain essential information. The leader and the organization's chief inspector and auditor should have a close relationship. It is important for the chief inspector and auditor to tell only the whole and unvarnished truth. The inspection systems within the organization must be manned with excellent people who, because of their recognized competence, have the respect of individuals at all levels. The inspection system must emphasize integrity and not deteriorate into a pattern of activity which encourages prevarications and the withholding of important information. Self-inspection systems within subordinate organizations also can be effective tools. The leader should show interest in and support for such systems and ask for periodic reports on problem areas uncovered by these self-inspection systems.

Management control systems, which allow a great deal of quantifiable data to reach the leader, are also useful feedback mechanisms. However, in their worst forms, they can become heavy burdens on subordinate organizations, detract from the mission, and deteriorate into exercises in data manipulation and dishonest reporting. A leader who has a computer on the desk where all kinds of information within the organization can be called up should never feel secure that the information is timely or accurate. If the information in this computer system is found to be inaccurate or dishonest, the leader should shut down the system or take corrective action to be sure the information flow becomes an effective means to help lead and manage the organization. A leader should periodically have an outside agency examine the management control system in detail to be sure it is serving the desires of the leader and the mission of the organization.

Informal feedback through individuals who are not in the organizational hierarchy and who do not work directly for the top leader also can be effective. Retired individuals who are keeping in close touch with many of their friends who remain within the organization can be good sources of mature and objective feedback. The "spouses' net" can provide valuable insights. Additionally, there are almost always individuals who are so "tuned in" that they can be helpful even though they do not occupy key positions within the hierarchical structure. For instance, some of the best information might come from an individual who works in the base gymnasium. As the basketball coach for the base team, he may have marvelous contacts and insights into morale problems, drug or alcohol difficulties, integrity problems, etc. Excellent feedback from the choir master of the chapel program and from the community relations specialist can assist leaders in knowing what is going on in their organization.

Leaders should be careful how they use these informal means of feedback. They must support subordinate leaders and must not violate the established rules of hierarchy. On the other hand, not utilizing informal means of feedback can be a mistake. Without good feedback from many sources, the leader of a large organization is partially blind and, over time, can become isolated from the real problems and the real issues. Isolation diminishes a leader's ability to anticipate problems, to receive innovative ideas, to maximize opportunities, and to serve as an enlightened and creative leader.

11/REACHING OUTWARD AND UPWARD:
responsibilities

IT IS IMPORTANT FOR the leaders of large organizations not only to know their people and their missions well, to plan carefully and to manage the solution of problems within the organization, but also to reach out to other organizations, to higher headquarters, to sister units, to the outside community and to institutions which have important interactions with the organization. A leader should spend a considerable amount of time building bridges.

A useful formula to be followed is to treat sister organizations with warmth, respect, and affection. A leader is not serving the organization well if there are turf battles with neighboring institutions. If the top leader figuratively embraces the leaders of major bureaucratic rivals and lets everyone in the organization know that criticism, backbiting or turf battles will not be tolerated, many of the problems that exist between organizations will quickly disappear—whether it be the relationship between a mayor and the city council, between the planners and the programmers in the Pentagon, between the Army or the Air Force or between the Department of Defense and the Department of State. When leaders pledge themselves to work cooperatively, they reduce considerably the risk of highly competitive individuals turning good, honest competition into dysfunctional criticism, parochialism and unproductive opposition.

In working with higher headquarters, the leader must be loyal to those above him, knowledgeable concerning the key agencies and department heads, and cooperative with the staff members. The leader must keep an eye on those staff members and agencies at higher headquarters who ask unreasonable things of people, put unwarranted pressures on the organization, and operate as if they were the ultimate leader. It is also important for leaders of organizations at lower levels to stand up for their people, to contact the staff agencies who are placing undue requirements on them, and to set standards for interaction that are appropriate within the chain of command. Doing this delicately, and with mutual respect, is a difficult job, but one which leaders must address. It has been my experience that superiors want to know how their staff and subordinate commands are working together. By raising problem areas and making appropriate suggestions for improvement through the chain of command, leader to leader, higher headquarters will be responsive and, in fact, appreciative of the input.

At the higher levels of very large organizations, outreach becomes almost an art form. The chemistry that develops between you, as a leader, and your boss greatly affects the relationship between the staff of the boss, your staff, and your subordinate organizations. If you can maintain an atmosphere of mutual trust and respect between you and your boss, as well as with top staff people, your subordinates will benefit. If, however, the chemistry between you and your boss is bad or if the staff is constantly "poisoning your well," you and your subordinates are in for a rough time. If your organization performs most of its duties, tasks, and missions in an outstanding way, trust and good chemistry are fairly easy to establish and maintain in most cases. It is your role to work hard to maintain that good chemistry between your organization and the next higher echelon.

Of course, leaders must be careful not to consider outreach their major objective. There are some leaders who spend so much time satisfying the boss above them, doing so much outreach to other organizations, and spending disproportionate amounts of time on diplomatic functions, that they spend too little time with the organizations they lead. These individuals become absentee leaders and, as a result, begin to lose the loyalty and support of the people who work for them. It is the mature leader who keeps outreach and "inreach" in proper balance. As in so many areas of leadership, what you do or how you do it is important, but so is a proper sense of proportion and balance.

12/UNDERSTANDING PERSONALITY TYPES:
a tool for enlightened leaders

IN RECENT YEARS, THERE have been some very useful innovations in the area of leadership development. Many institutions of higher learning, such as Harvard University, offer specialized programs aimed at the leadership needs of senior managers in business and the federal government. An important part of these executive development courses is an assessment activity which administers a series of sophisticated tests designed to evaluate the various skills, personality preferences, and leadership styles of the participants. The assessments offer the participants a unique set of insights into their various strengths and weaknesses. The courses then afford them the opportunity to learn new skills which help to promote their strengths, and assist in correcting their weaknesses.

One of the most popular assessment instruments is the *Myers Briggs Type Indicator* (MBTI). The MBTI, which is published by the Consulting Psychologists Press, is based upon the typology of Carl Jung. The instrument measures personality styles and preferences along four continuums which further separate into sixteen categories. The categories further differentiate themselves based on the strengths of an individual's scores. The first continuum evaluates the individual in terms of extroversion or introversion. Jung, who invented these two terms, felt that this continuum represented the most powerful differences between people. The extrovert (E) thinks out loud in the world of people and things, while the introvert (I) processes information internally in the world of concepts and ideas. The second continuum deals with the ways that individuals gather information for the decisionmaking process. The first difference is called sensing (S), because these individuals gather data with the five basic senses. The second difference on this continuum is referred to as intuition (N) because these individuals prefer to leap over the tangibles and look for hidden meanings, relationships, and possibilities. The third continuum deals with opposite ways of deciding. The first preference is called thinking (T). These individuals make decisions fairly impersonally based upon an evaluation of cause and effect. The other end of this third continuum is called feeling (F), in which individuals with this style tend to make decisions based on personal values. The fourth and final continuum is the only dimension that is not directly drawn from Jungian theory, although it certainly complements it. This continuum, developed by the two authors of the MBTI, deals with differences between people in the use of perception and the use of judgment in dealing with the outer world. Individuals with the judging (J) preference rely on a judging process, and tend to live in a planned, decided, orderly manner. They seek constantly to regulate and control their lives. The perceptive (P) individuals rely mainly on a perceptive process for dealing with the outer world, and live in a flexible and spontaneous manner. Their quest in life is understanding the meaning of life, and adapting to it. These four continuums in combination with one another make up the sixteen MBTI types.

The following tables,* taken from the book, *Please Understand Me: An Essay on Temperament Styles* by David Keirsey and Marilyn Bates, illustrate the differences that are measured by the MBTI.

E (75% of the population)	*versus* I (25% of the population)
Sociability	Territoriality
Interaction	Concentration
External	Internal
Breadth	Depth
Extensive	Intensive
Multiplicity of relationships	Limited relationships
Expenditure of energies	Conservation of energies
Interest in external events	Interest in internal reaction

*David Keirsey and Marilyn Bates, *Please Understand Me: An Essay on Temperament Styles* (Del Mar, CA: Prometheus Nemesis Books, 1978). Copyright © 1978, David Keirsey and Marilyn Bates. Reprinted by permission.

S (75% of the population)	versus	N (25% of the population)
Experience		Hunches
Past		Future
Realistic		Speculative
Perspiration		Inspiration
Actual		Possible
Down-to-earth		Head-in-clouds
Utility		Fantasy
Fact		Fiction
Practicality		Ingenuity
Sensible		Imaginative

T (50% of the population)	versus	F (50% of the population)
Objective		Subjective
Principles		Values
Policy		Social values
Laws		Extenuating circumstances
Criterion		Intimacy
Firmness		Persuasion
Impersonal		Personal
Justice		Humane
Categories		Harmony
Standards		Good or bad
Critique		Appreciate
Analysis		Sympathy
Allocation		Devotion

J (50% of the population)	versus	P (50% of the population)
Settled		Pending
Decided		Gather more data
Fixed		Flexible
Plan ahead		Adapt as you go
Run one's life		Let life happen
Closure		Open options
Decision-making		Treasure hunting
Planned		Open ended
Completed		Emergent
Decisive		Tentative
Wrap it up		Something will turn up
Urgency		There's plenty of time
Deadline!		What deadline?
Get show on the road		Let's wait and see

Another instrument, not well known to date, is called the *Kirton Adaption-Innovation Inventory* (KAI).* Authored by Michael J. Kirton of the Occupational Research Center, Hatfield Polytechnic, Hertfordshire, England, the theory contends that people differ in the manner in which they define and solve problems because of a preference for either being "Adaptive" or "Innovative" in their approach to change. The scores range from 32 to 160. A score of 32 to 80 would place an individual in the "adaptor" range. A score between 81 to 113 places individuals in a middle range called "bridgers." And scores between 114 and 160 are characterized as "innovators." Sixty-seven percent of those people who take the instrument score as a "bridger." The following chart, adapted from Kirton's writings, shows the differences between people on this instrument.

CHARACTERISTICS OF ADAPTORS AND INNOVATORS

Implications	Adaptors	Innovators
Problem Solving	Tend to take the problem as defined and generate novel, creative ideas aimed at "doing things better"	Tend to redefine generally agreed problems, breaking previously perceived restraints, generating solutions aimed at "doing things differently"

*Copyright M.J. Kirton 1985, Reprinted with the permission of M.J. Kirton 1986, Occupational Research Centre, The Hatfield Polytechnic, Hertfordshire AL10AB, England.

Implications	Adaptors	Innovators
Solutions	Generate a few well chosen and relevant solutions, that they find sufficient but generally fail to contain ideas that break the existing patterns completely	Produce ideas that may not be obvious or acceptable. Pool of ideas can crack intractable problems
Policies	Prefer well established, structured situations. Best at incorporating new data or events into existing structures or policies	Prefer unstructured situations. See opportunities to set new structures or policies with attendant risk
Organizational Fit	Essential for ongoing functions. May have trouble changing established role in time of needed change	Essential in time of change or crisis. May have trouble applying themselves to ongoing organizational needs
Perceived Behavior	Seen by Innovators as sound, conforming, safe, predictable, relevant, inflexible, wedded to the system, intolerant of ambiguity	Seen by Adaptors as unsound, impracticable, risky, abrasive, often shocking their opposites, and creating dissonance

The KAI is often misunderstood. It is *not* a measure of creativity. It is a measure of an individual's style of creativity: his or her capacity for creative problem solving. Both adaptors and innovators are capable of generating original and creative solutions to complex and difficult problems. The instrument simply measures their preferences and differences in their approach to problem solving. The KAI gives those who take the test the opportunity to understand their decisionmaking style.

Bridgers are needed to appreciate the differences between the adaptors and the innovators. Adaptors work very well within established organizations, but may become too structured and bound by organizational or bureaucratic constraints. They need to be challenged to move outside the system on occasion. The innovators need even more nurturing. One of the first reactions of some leaders would be to try to mold their behavior to the culture of the organization. While some of this may be necessary to conduct routine business, the innovators, if given some latitude, can provide valuable insights and potential for growth.

A third useful test, the creation of Dr. Elias H. Porter, is the *Strength Deployment Inventory*. Though not yet well known, Porter's work is growing in popularity. Porter's test provides additional understanding and insights into one's individual behavior, and that of others. The instrument measures behavior, first under normal stress-free conditions, and, second, when the individual perceives conflict and opposition. These two scores are then displayed in a manner wherein the individuals can see their scores on a multi-dimensional continuum. While there are various possible combinations, the SDI indicates interpersonal styles clustered around the following orientations:

Altruistic-Nurturing

The basic value system of these individuals is a genuine concern for the protection, growth, and personal welfare of others. They strive to be open and responsive to the needs of others. This style is color coded *blue.*

Analytic-Autonomizing

These individuals value the importance of a rational, analytical process and order. Their style is to be objective, in control of their emotions, cautious and thorough, fair and principled, and thinking things through before acting. They are color coded *green* on the instrument.

Assertive-Directing

The primary value system of these individuals is a concern for task accomplishment and the organization of people and associated resources toward that end. Their style is toward leadership and persuasion, alert for opportunities, quick to claim the right to earned rewards, inclined to push for immediate action. They will challenge others, and will relish risk taking. They are color coded *red* on the SDI.

Flexible-Cohering

This preference is a blend of the other three styles. They are not identified by a color and are referred to as *hubs* (or rainbows) since they are a true combination of all three. They are oriented to the importance of membership in groups and effective group behavior. They are curious about what others think and feel, are open-minded, and are willing to adapt and change. These individuals like to experiment with how to act, like to be members of groups, and like to be known as flexible.

Most people who take the Strength Deployment Inventory do not score in one of the four pure orientations described above. They find themselves to be combinations and mixes in a less pure form.

The Strength Deployment Inventory is useful because it categorizes individual orientations into groupings that are easy to understand. The most interesting insight that comes out of the SDI, in my judgment, is what happens to individuals when they are confronted or criticized. Behavior orientation often changes. For instance in my case, I am a Red-Blue which means that I am a hard-driving, goal-setting, ambitious person, but I also have some altruistic, caring qualities. My goal-setting qualities are more prominent than the altruistic qualities. When confronted, I turn Green which is the analytical orientation. I generally don't get mad, I get interested, if someone criticizes me. It allows me to handle criticism somewhat less emotionally than people who turn Red when they are confronted and become angry. Those who turn Blue during conflict work hard to accommodate the criticism, to compromise, and to find ways to end the confrontation as soon as possible. If they cannot find accommodation, they will try to withdraw.

One of the newest evaluation devices is the "hot reactor" test which measures the relationship between psychological stress and physiological reactivity. The procedure looks at the relationship between stress and blood pressure. About 25 percent of American executives, when placed under mild psychological stress, have very high blood pressure readings. The procedure was developed by Dr.

91

Robert Eliot, who is the Director of Preventative and Rehabilitative Cardiology at the Heart-Lung Center, St. Luke's Hospital in Phoenix, Arizona. The "hot reactor" test takes about 45 minutes to administer. The subject is connected to an automatic blood pressure machine then asked to engage in a series of mental activities. The performance on the assigned tasks is recorded as well as the blood pressures. A significant number of individuals exhibit high blood pressures during these activities which are significantly different from their resting blood pressures. The procedure gives the subject an indication of what his actual blood pressure is during normal day-to-day activities. Leaders who fully understand the implications of the "hot reactor" test can do a great service to those subordinates who are doing major physical damage to themselves as a result of their reactions to ringing telephones, angry bosses, short deadlines, etc. These individuals can be helped with medical interventions, and changes in work patterns and life styles. Leaders who are interested in the health of their organizations and the wellness of the people who work for them should learn about the "hot reactor" test, and, if possible, make it available for subordinates.

It is clear from available and proven tests that physical and mental health are closely related. People who are in regular exercise programs and who maintain good control of their work habits, diet, and weight, have more to contribute in the long term to the goals of their institutions than those who are very overweight, or who do not pay attention to their diet and health habits and, therefore, often work below potential performance levels. Treadmill stress tests, in coordination with a blood chemistry analysis, can determine quite precisely the "health age" of an individual. A fifty-year-old person who has a health-age of sixty-five may not contribute to an organization for many more years unless corrective action, with regard to diet, exercise, excessive smoking and drinking, is taken soon. Leaders themselves should also take these tests since the health of the leader has a great deal to do with the health of the organization. Also, by taking the tests, a leader shows interest in, and support for, the fitness program.

There is a close relationship between physical and mental health and between physical and mental vigor. For instance, many do their best thinking while walking or jogging, returning from their exercise with new vigor to attack the issues of the day, as well as with new ideas. If leaders are visible to subordinates as they pursue their exercise programs, they are likely to encourage others to get regular exercise. Look carefully at the exercise facilities available to subordinates: locker rooms and shower facilities, exercise rooms and intramural sports programs. Attention to this area can reap great benefits in performance and morale, as well as in mental and physical fitness.

In addition to understanding individual psychological and physical factors, a wise leader will periodically examine the psychological climate of the organization. For instance, the National War College has an educational climate and a curriculum which heavily emphasize extroversion and intuition. Active learning (emphasized in the seminar environment), case study approaches, and political-military simulations all favor the extrovert. The emphasis on conceptualization, frameworks of analysis, and models in the curriculum favors the intuitive personality over the sensing personality. Since about half of our students are neither extroverts nor intuitives, they are somewhat disadvantaged by this educational approach. By recognizing our bias in favor of individuals whose personality preferences favor extroversion and intuition, the faculty has taken an important first step. The next step is more difficult: redesigning the academic program to accommodate the needs and desires of the introverts and sensors while preserving the excellence of the present program.

13/LOOKING AT
YOURSELF:
the importance of introspection

LEADERS SHOULD THINK
of themselves as individuals surrounded by mirrors
of many kinds. Many of these mirrors are distorted;
some of them reflect back so leaders can judge themselves, but many of them do not. Even the most consistent of leaders is many things to many people.
Leaders should try to correct the worst of these dis-
tortions when possible. However, they must avoid
becoming paranoid or defensive about the distor-
tions they cannot correct. Herein lies the need for
self-confidence and self-esteem combined with the
willingness to listen, to accept criticism, to learn from
mistakes. Leaders must realize that they are three
people: who they are, who they think they are, and
who they are perceived to be by their subordinates,
peers, and superiors. In many cases, there is a close
relationship between and among the three "yous." In

other cases, the relationship is not close at all. Just as you are not as handsome, sexy, brilliant, witty, or charismatic as you sometimes think you are, you may well be perceived in much less favorable light than the facts would support. If you very occasionally have one too many drinks, you will be perceived by many as a chronic alcoholic; if you occasionally close your eyes or nod off during a long, boring meeting, you will be perceived by many as suffering from incipient senility. If you occasionally fire a subordinate, you will be perceived as a leader who is constantly on the watch to find someone to fire. The true mature leader acknowledges these "perception gaps" and works hard to become introspective and to get feedback, and to take corrective action when appropriate.

A leader of an organization needs to be introspective. This introspection process should be accomplished systematically; it should be done regularly; and, it should be done with the help of someone else, whether it be the leader's executive secretary, deputy, executive assistant, trusted friend, or spouse.

Establishing your schedule. How much time do you spend visiting on the shop floor, in the manufacturing and maintenance areas, or in the field? How much time do you spend with your subordinates watching or playing organized sports or participating in informal sports such as jogging? Do you attend social gatherings? Does your secretary keep a close track of your schedule and provide feedback as to how many hours each month you are spending in such aspects of your job? How many hours are you spending visiting subordinate and subsidiary units, or attending meetings? What kind of meetings are they and who else attends those meetings? In my view, the four-hour rule, which recommends that leaders of large organizations should spend no more than four hours a day in the office, has great merit. The rest of the time should be spent meeting with other people, visiting subsidiary organizations, participating in or watching sports activities with subordinates, attending social events, conducting ceremonies, or giving short, substantive, motivational speeches.

Henry Brandon of the London *Times* made a critical point which has relevance for leaders of large organizations, "Americans tend to be influenced in their judgment of politicians and corporate executives by how much time they spend behind their desks. They do not attach enough importance to the advantages of the clarity of a relaxed mind."

Establishing your priorities. Do you and your people know what your priorities are? Have you written them down and discussed them with your subordinates? Do you follow your own priorities? Individuals in top leadership positions need to establish priorities for themselves and for their organization. There should be a close correlation between the priorities of the individual in a leadership position and the priorities of the organization. After these priorities are articulated both in oral and written form, they should be followed by the leader. If you establish priorities that you are unwilling to follow, those priorities become a source of cynical comment.

Examining your reliability. How often do you cancel out at the last minute on a meeting, speech, ceremony, visit, sporting event, or social engagement? Once you make a commitment to do something, you should do it. Only an emergency, ill health, or some other serious crisis should cause you to cancel a commitment. Of course, in agreeing to do things, you should be careful not to over-schedule yourself, not to accept responsibilities that you, in fact, can't fulfill, and not to doublebook a specific period. In Europe, I was impressed by the great respect the senior leaders from many nations had for the then Supreme Allied Commander in Europe, General Alexander M. Haig, Jr. When they were asked individually why they had such high regard for General Haig, the answer was always along the following lines, "Al Haig is reliable. If he says he is going to put a United States brigade in northern Germany, he puts a brigade in there. If he says he's going to make a speech for me, he makes a speech for me. If he says he's going to visit a certain unit, he visits that unit. Whether he's tired, whether he's sick, or whether he has other things on his mind, he lives up to his commitments. Al Haig is reliable and I respect him for that."

Who tells you all the news—good and bad? It is important for leaders to have around them people who are honest and forthright, who give them the bad news as well as the good news, and who do not play the role of sycophants when dealing with them. You need to sit down periodically and ask yourself, who around me is willing to tell the full story? Is it your deputy, your executive officer, your secretary, a trusted friend, your spouse, or your children? If there is no one, or if those voices are very weak, you should hire someone and put him or her very close to you so that you have someone to tell you when the "emperor has no clothes."

How long are your meetings? If you love to hear your own voice, your meetings can go on for hours and there is an enormous amount of time wasted for you and your key subordinates. Meetings should be short, brisk, and to the point with a reasonable agenda set ahead of time and followed. A good basic rule on routine meetings is that they should not last more than one hour and, if there is to be a briefing, there should be no more than 20 slides used. If there is more than an hour's worth of business to be done, the meeting should be broken into parts. Long meetings are dysfunctional, tying up people and straining the attention span of many. You need to look at yourself and find out whether you or your subordinates have become, as many leaders do, enamored with your own words. Do you preach rather than listen?

How well do you listen? Listening is an acquired art. It requires self-discipline and well developed skills. Leaders should listen and listen and listen. Only through listening can they find out what's really going on. If someone comes in to raise an issue with the leader and the leader does not allow the individual to state the full case and to get emotions out on the table, the leader is likely to understand only a piece of the story and the problem probably will not be solved. In addition, the individual who brought in the problem will be frustrated because there was no opportunity to lay the whole issue on the table and to make sure the leader fully understood the problem. Passive listening is important at times when the individual wants to get something off his/her chest and doesn't want to be interrupted; active listening also can be very useful for the leader to make sure one tracks what is being said, to make sure the case is stated clearly and to permit good communications on both sides. It is a judgment call about whether the leader should be a passive listener or an active listener, but both should be done and, when in doubt, err on the side of passive rather than active listening.

Do people fear you, distrust you, like you, respect you, love you? What do people think about you? Are they comfortable with you or are they afraid of you? Do they feel they can really tell it like it is, or do they withhold information for fear that you might explode, overreact, or make judgments about them that might be lasting and wrong? What people feel about you is important for you as a leader. If they feel good about you and if they respect and admire you, you are much more likely to have good communication with them, thereby enhancing your productivity as a leader. It is useful to remind oneself of the old adage: friends come and go, but enemies accumulate. Your spouse, children, old friends, and trusted subordinates can really help with this. You should ask them often the Mayor (of New York City) Ed Koch question, "How am I doing?"

What is your body language like? What is your office demeanor? Do you sit behind your desk and pontificate or are you willing to get away from the desk? Do you show a certain defensive nature in your body language? Are you able, literally and figuratively, to wrap your arms around people? Do people feel that they can break through the interpersonal barriers that exist between subordinate and boss when discussing an issue with you? How visibly approachable are you? Many visible leaders are not approachable and don't realize how their demeanor makes people reluctant to approach them.

Are you considered to be a communicator? Do you help your people to learn, understand, and develop? How well do you speak? Do you make brief speeches that are to the point? Do you mix humor in with your speeches? How well and how often do you write? How well do you dictate and edit?

Are you considered to be a disciplinarian? If so, are you a benign disciplinarian or a harsh disciplinarian? Do you take time to counsel people? Do you ever fire anyone? For what reasons and in what style? Do you counsel people before you relieve them of their responsibilities? Leaders who are tough, but fair, who don't confuse leniency with leadership, and who don't appear at extremes of being too easy or too harsh, normally serve their institution well. Individuals in organizations want a leader who is a fair disciplinarian, who does not fire without careful consideration, and who sets standards for the unit that the leader also is willing to follow.

Do you enjoy your job? By letting people know that you are enjoying your job, you can help create a healthy atmosphere in your organization. Leaders who enjoy their jobs, and show everyone they do, often help their subordinates enjoy their jobs as well. Do you feel genuine joy in the successes of your subordinates?

Are you an innovator? Are you someone who hangs on to the status quo, or is caught in policy rigidities that do not allow much flexibility? General Matthew Ridgway, the great combat leader of World War II and Korea, made a very telling point after he retired from the US Army: "My greatest contribution as Chief of Staff was nourishing the mavericks." Are you someone who is open to suggestions, ideas, new thoughts, new directions and new concepts? On the other hand, are you someone who innovates too much and creates turmoil within the organization because you are constantly changing your mind on policies, organizations, personnel, and other issues? Have you the proper balance between continuity and creativity? In some situations, a great deal of innovation is needed and accepted. In other situations, innovation must be pushed slowly and incrementally to not destroy the existing strength of the organization. How well do you maintain this balance?

Are you flexible? Are you an individual so rigid in your thinking and life-style that you are not open to ideas? Conversely, are you flexible to a fault? Do you swing with the breeze? Once you make up your mind, are you willing to stick with your decision unless strong and compelling arguments are made to change your mind? How do you fit on the continuum between too much flexibility and not enough?

Do you maintain physical and intellectual fitness? Do you show some interest in maintaining physical fitness or are you too busy or too disinclined to get involved in sporting activities? It is in your interest as a leader of a large organization to encourage people to have some time for physical fitness and recreation. If you are a non-athlete and you are not interested in fitness, you should, at least, consider that an athletic program may be very useful to the organization. Are you intellectually fit? Do you have a reading program? Do you bring in consultants and futurists to stretch your mind?

Are you a deflector of pressure from above or a magnifier of that pressure? One of the roles of a leader is to accept guidance and criticism in a mature way. If you are constantly magnifying the pressure that comes from your superiors and putting more and more pressure on your subordinates as a result, you may be doing a disservice to organizational morale and your mission. At times, a leader should deflect these pressures; at other times, a leader should let some of these pressures flow through the organization.

Are you tuned in or are you out of touch? Leaders who get isolated in their office or who don't have the ability to reach out and find out what's really going on, soon get a reputation for being out of touch. What are the means you use for staying tuned in? Are your antennas out all the time? Do you have good feedback mechanisms?

Are you a delegator? There are many bosses who run their entire organization from the front office. These types tend to be individuals with enormous amounts of energy and intellect. Unfortunately, such individuals do not help subordinates develop into future leaders. Leaders who often delegate authority are not only encouraging leadership at lower levels, but are also giving people a great deal of psychic reward. However, a leader should not be so aggressive in the desire to delegate that he/she loses touch and becomes nothing more than a traffic cop. Overdelegation can lead to the "Balkanization" of an organization, where no one is in charge. People who are willing to delegate rather liberally are probably doing a good job of creating a healthy organization that can carry on effectively if they should become disabled, incapacitated, or replaced by a less competent individual. A major aspect of delegation is empowerment. The top leader should empower subordinates so they have full authority to decide without checking with the top leader. Many leaders delegate conditionally when they should empower unconditionally.

Are you a non-drinker, a drinker, or an alcoholic? Occasionally a leader who had a mild drinking problem prior to taking over leadership responsibilities drifts into a more heavy drinking pattern that may lead to alcoholism or, at least, to a serious drinking problem. The pressures of leadership are sometimes quite severe, and individuals who have psychological or health problems relating to alcohol abuse often find their problems exacerbated. With regard to alcohol, you need to ask yourself some questions: Now that I'm a leader, what should be my approach to alcohol consumption? How am I viewed by others? The perception of alcoholism of the leader is often as important as the reality of alcoholism in the environment of a large organization.

Are you an optimist or a pessimist? If you are constantly optimistic to the point of being a Pollyanna, you may lose the respect of people because you are unable to acknowledge the seamy side of your organization or to see the tough problems because you always have on your rose-colored glasses. On the other hand, if you are constantly pessimistic and cynical, morale in your organization can suffer. A pragmatically optimistic individual, who is not a Pollyanna but comes to work with a lot of enthusiasm and optimism, tends to be an effective and respected leader. Although a cynic might do a good job as a leader, this cynicism and pessimism may soon negatively transfer throughout the organization.

Are you religious? What are your ethics and values? Do you go to religious services; do you ever mention religious or moral values in your speeches or in your writings? If you attend religious services, do you ever become an active participant? When there is a funeral in your organization, are you ever asked to participate in the service? Have you ever been asked to stand up in front of a religious group and give a speech? Many people who work for you will watch you in terms of whether you are committed to their ethics and values. They will hope for someone as a leader who shares those values. You should be wary, however, about the danger of seeming to inflict your religious standards on others. Leaders who are, or appear to be, self-righteous often fail to gain or maintain good rapport with a large number of subordinates.

Are you a writer? Do you write a column in the weekly newspaper? How well do you write or endorse employee evaluations? Do you write letters? Do you write them well and with style? If you are a poor writer, you may unintentionally harm your people in many ways. When it is time for you to write a letter of recommendation for someone who has done an excellent job for you and the letter lacks punch, you are failing that individual. If you write poor evaluation reports, you are also doing individuals a disservice. If you are a poor writer you should get someone to help you. Get your executive officer, your deputy or your public affairs officer to help you with your writing, to edit your writing to clean it up, to make it "punchy," to make it clearer. If you learn to write well, you can better serve your organization and your efforts will be appreciated.

Are you ambitious? Are you personally ambitious, or are you ambitious for your subordinates and your organization? In what way do your ambitions come through? A number of people who have moved to top positions in our government in recent years have been so personally ambitious that they sometimes forgot a leader's first responsibility is to the mission and goals of the organization and the country.

Are you secure or are you insecure? If you are a person who is secure within, knowing your own capabilities and your own weaknesses, comfortable with yourself and with your basic life-style, not tending to be defensive and able to accept criticism well, you can serve as a mature leader in many different positions. If you are basically insecure and worry a great deal about your performance and your ability to do the job, you may have a more difficult task. As you mature as a leader, your sense of security should increase as your organization succeeds. Many initially insecure people who build their self-confidence over time can become mature, successful leaders. The leader's spouse can be very helpful in this regard by praising the leader's strengths and accomplishments, particularly when the leader is having problems with the organization and is not receiving much praise or support from other sources. Conversely, a spouse can do much good by taking the leader down a peg or two if the leader's ego becomes overly inflated.

Are you a philanderer? Some leaders pursue the thrills of conquest. Moral issues aside, leaders must recognize that they are being watched very carefully. If they are in the military, they are being observed by their command post, security police, secretary, executive officer, and subordinates. The word quickly gets out that the boss is looking for the next liaison. A number of leaders in government have been fired for the simple reason that they would not control their libido.

What is your integrity level? Leaders must realize that personal integrity and institutional integrity meet in the front office. If you have a commitment to integrity, both personal and institutional, if you talk about it, write about it, mean it, and live it, there is a good chance that institutional integrity and personal integrity throughout the organization will remain high. If, however, you are not concerned about integrity and are willing to allow the rules to be bent, institutional integrity may degenerate rapidly.

Are you an intense individual or are you relaxed? What kind of demeanor do you project as you enter meetings, carry on conversations, and make speeches? Are you able to relax, or do the burdens and responsibilities of leadership cause you to have an intense air about you most of the time? Do you sit on the front edge of your chair? Do you interrupt

107

people when they are trying to tell you something? These signals can help you determine your level of intensity and may help you evaluate whether your intensity adds to, or detracts from, your success as a leader.

Are you decisive or are you a "decision ducker"? Some wag once said, there are three types of people: those that make things happen, those that watch things happen, and those who wonder what happened. Top leaders should follow the 60 percent rule, which states that when you have about 60 percent of the information that you need to make a decision, you should make it, because if you wait much longer to get more information you will miss some key decision points. Thus, a leader has to be both decisive and willing to make decisions without all the facts. Leaders who constantly duck decisions that should be made create an atmosphere of non-decisiveness and the organization tends to float. Too often, decisions that should be made by the boss tend to be made by lower level people and often without full coordination. If top level decisions are always left to subordinates, many of those decisions will be very good, but consistency and coherency of policy often suffer. If you prefer to have other people within your organization make most of the decisions, you should at least ensure that there is a general consistency on policy with full coordination.

How conceptual are you? Are you able to put the mission, goals, requirements, and responsibilities of your organization in a conceptual framework? Are you able to explain that conceptual framework to other people? A leader who conceptualizes well is usually a good planner and an excellent teacher.

Executive Menopause. Most leaders do not reach positions of great responsibility until they reach their 40s or early 50s. If they have climbed up the military or corporate ladder, these leaders may have become used to working very long hours, with little time for a systematic physical exercise program, and they may have developed poor habits of diet and heavy smoking. Executive burnout is a rather common phenomenon for individuals of this type. This burnout can be avoided by careful time management, good control of diet and smoking, and a regular exercise program whereby vigorous exercise three or four times a week becomes an integral part of the weekly schedule. Another aspect of executive menopause is the tendency of some leaders to be seduced by "perks." Company airplanes, free homes, magnificent offices, superb outer office support, opportunities to travel widely, can all, in an insidious way, divert the attention of the leader from the mission.

When considering military leadership, J.F.C. Fuller's classic small book, *Generalship: Its Diseases and Their Cures*, makes the point that the best generalship in war occurs between the ages of 34 and 45 because combat leadership requires the physical strength, courage, stamina, flexibility, and risk-taking more often found in younger men and seldom found in men past the age of 50. He examined 100 great military leaders of history and found that at the time of their greatest triumph they tended to be quite young (74 percent were 45 or younger). Although Fuller's book was written before World War II, it seems to endorse the present personnel philosophy of the United States military, which has most senior officers retiring in their late 40s or early 50s.

Avoiding the Paul Principle. Whereas the Peter Principle can be avoided by proper preparation for each higher level of responsibility, the Paul Principle can also be avoided through hard work and good planning. The Paul Principle is the gradual obsolescence of leaders as they lose touch with the organization they lead, become too conservative, resist innovation and change, and fail to take advantage of technological breakthroughs. A systematic reading program, participation in management training symposia or workshops, regular interaction with long-range planners, and brainstorming activities with the staff can all help to repeal the Paul Principle.

The Red Reactor Problem. Those leaders who react emotionally or violently to criticism from below often fail as leaders because, over time, they lose touch with the organizations they are charged to lead. They also tend to lose some of their best subordinates who, out of frustration, move on to other places where constructive criticism and healthy debate are part of the corporate climate. Leaders who take criticism poorly damage vital feedback mechanisms and may cause subordinates to jump ship. When such leaders face crises, they will look futilely for the creative subordinate who could have bailed them out. Over time, such leaders also have difficulty recruiting talented individuals, for the word quickly spreads that the top leader is unreceptive to criticism. A particularly unfortunate quality in a leader is a combination of poor reaction to criticism and a tendency to hold grudges. Those individuals who know they are "Red Reactors" and who receive criticism poorly should strive to constrain this personality preference; at the same time, they should look for individuals with enough self-confidence not to be intimidated by an occasional outburst by the leader.

If leaders are introspective and get help from close colleagues, they can serve as better leaders. They also can avoid some mistakes and portray the aura of leadership which, in turn, elicits both the respect of subordinates and support for a leader's initiatives.

14/DEALING WITH THE MEDIA:
the challenge and the opportunity

THE MEDIA CAN PROVIDE an opportunity for a leader to compliment and thank others, and to get proper recognition for the organization and its people. Therefore, the leader should seek out the media and try to bring them in to write stories and produce television shows or clips in support of the organization's goals and to highlight the accomplishments of individuals. Leaders should not take the attitude that the media is the enemy, that the press cannot be trusted, or that the best policy is to avoid any contact with them. In general, the media can be helpful. It is important, though, to maintain an attitude of skepticism because you may periodically be burned by some members of the media, whether you call them in or not. It is important to be accurate in what you say to members of the media and to avoid making statements that can be easily taken out of context or misquoted.

It is useful to establish ground rules in each contact with the media. Will this interview be on or off the record? Will you have the opportunity to see the manuscript or the videotape before it goes final? If not, why not? It is generally useful to speak informally with the reporter before you get into the formal interview to find out whether that reporter has any major preconceptions or misconceptions. If so, you can try to rectify such misunderstanding. If you cannot, you should be particularly wary of what you say because, when media representatives have already made up their minds, it is often a question of trying to "limit damage" as much as possible. If a member of the media is clearly biased and is not likely to do a fair story, you have a responsibility to alert your bosses and the public affairs people at higher levels to let them know that a critical article or program is coming, despite your best efforts.

If the reporter is willing to show the manuscript to you before it goes to press, you can clear up some misconceptions, correct errors that might have been made, help expand some points that need expanding, and so forth. Many responsible journalists will allow you to help them if you have established a sense of mutual respect and an understanding of the importance of telling the story correctly and accurately. Joking with the media, relaxing with them, giving them the opportunity to observe first hand what your organization does, giving them the chance to see some things that they would not normally see, and to talk to people with whom they would not normally have contact are some useful techniques to consider. These techniques can ensure an accurate media insight into your organization and establish appropriate rapport with the influential news profession, breaking down the natural barriers that often exist between people in government and the media.

When a media visit is imminent, a leader can run stories in the company or installation newspaper telling the readers that ABC News or the *New York Times* or the *Economist* is coming to do a story. The leader can explain that the media's interest is a compliment. The presence of the media can be used as a motivating and uplifting experience for members of your unit. If you can get the story out ahead of time, you can show the members of the press that you have, in fact, alerted your subordinates that they are coming, that you are happy that they are there, and that you have encouraged candor in answering their questions. You may consequently establish a good rapport between working members of the press and yourself which can carry on for years.

Often, when members of the media ask questions of a leader, they don't ask the best questions. If you feel comfortable in dealing with members of the media who are asking the questions, you can often steer them in the right direction. If they ask a question that is not particularly relevant, you can answer the question but follow up with, "That was a good question but I think there is a better question that you might have asked along the following lines." Then you ask the question and answer it yourself. This will educate the media representatives and hopefully they will pick up on your points. The interview can thus become more productive. Members of the media often spread themselves so thin across so many issues and so many places that they really don't know what questions to ask. You can help them ask the right questions. This technique can put you in charge of the interview and help to tell the story you want to tell.

The leader should have an agenda, a point of view or theme, that he wants to get across during the interview. He should answer the questions in such a way that his agenda comes across loud and clear. There is a story about Donald Rumsfeld when he was Secretary of Defense that illustrates this point. Rumsfeld was asked in a press interview how his mother was. Rumsfeld's reply was that she was fine but that she was worried about the Soviet threat!

A leader can use upcoming news conferences as a means to force subordinates to come up with recommended courses of action. For instance, President Kennedy used his biweekly press conference to accelerate the decisionmaking process, to keep informed on current issues, and to make policy decisions. In addition, speechwriters can be useful instruments in the decisionmaking process. In fact, official speeches are often the most important means by which decisions are announced. Leaders should ensure that there is a close relationship between their speechwriters and their public affairs specialists (as well as between those two groups and the key line and staff officials) so that interactions with the media and the general public can be as positive as possible.

Some large organizations have a media-training program for senior executives which gives them a chance to face various media opportunities in a well-simulated environment. In this training, the one-on-one interview, the general news conference, the confrontational news conference, the remote interview, and the speech followed by a question-and-answer format are all videotaped. The executive is then critiqued on style, body language, sense of humor, speaking voice, etc. Individuals who expect to move into top leadership jobs should take this training.

Although some have argued that America has developed into a massive adversary culture where disparagement by the media of all our institutions has become the norm, mature leaders can find ways to work positively with representatives of the news profession. Leaders of large organizations cannot hide from media representatives; they should stay in close touch with their public affairs officers and seek their guidance and support often.

15/CREATING A STRATEGIC VISION:
the role of planning

THE GREAT LEADERS OF our time have been not only effective operators and decisionmakers, but also people of vision who have had a marvelous sense of what was possible, how to set and articulate goals, and how to motivate their people to strive successfully for these goals. Great leaders tend to be great planners.

There are several important rules regarding the relationship between the leader and the planning staff. First, the leader must have direct access to the planners and should schedule time on a regular basis to meet with them. The leader must read, know, and understand the organization's most significant plans. Lastly, the leader has to be willing to exercise those operational plans periodically to allow the organization to practice important elements of these plans.

In all large organizations there needs to be a long-range planning group that prepares an overall long-range plan (updated annually) that addresses specific planning issues throughout the year. The leader must find time for a two-hour session with the long-range planners every month or two at which they can present their ideas and innovative solutions to long-range problems and expose the leader to the frontiers of developments in technology, concepts, doctrines, organizational theory, etc.

The annual long-range plan should be brief, usually about 10 to 12 pages. It should be signed by the top leader and should be distributed widely throughout the organization. The leader should refer to this plan periodically throughout the year. (Calling it "our strategic plan" is a useful technique.) Key subordinates should be assured that the leader will make decisions based on the strategic vision outlined in the long-range plan. If an organization has a strategic vision which includes specific goals and priorities developed in the long-range plan, day-to-day decisionmaking is much more likely to have real coherence. Goals can charge up people, can ignite the human spirit. If goals are carefully constructed and well understood, both good and bad luck can be better managed.

Another important element of planning is divestiture planning. All large organizations need to aggressively pursue divestiture strategies to ensure that they do not retain outdated or outmoded policies, doctrines, weapons systems, or research and development programs. Divestiture planning in business is normally easier to accomplish than divestiture planning in government. Economic analysis in a profitmaking firm normally points to areas of weakness and obsolescence within the organization. In government, divestiture is a more difficult process because the obsolete areas are harder to identify and more difficult to exorcise from the organization. The long-range planners can help in this regard by laying out an overall structure for the organization twenty years into the future. This helps the leader focus attention on areas that will not be relevant in the twenty-first century. By working in close coordination with long-range planners and a divestiture team, the leader can develop a scheme for phasing out those elements of the organization which would not be present in the next century. Divestiture should ideally take place before obsolescence sets in, before the organization, system, or doctrine is in decline. Preemptive divestiture should be the goal so that "coast artillery cannon" and "horse cavalries" of the future are phased out much earlier than they have been in the past. Divestiture teams must be carefully protected by the top leader. Many field agency and staff officials resent individuals who recommend initiatives for divestiture. Divestiture often means loss of jobs, power, and prestige. A leader must aggressively unload the "dogs" in the organization, but he must do so with the full understanding of the effect divestiture actions will have on the morale of his people.

As a new leader takes over a large organization, two of the most important questions are: "What is the long-range plan?" and "Who are the long-range planners?" If planners do not have direct access to you as a leader, reorganize to ensure that they do. If a leader of a large organization is not committed to an institutionalized planning process, the leader is likely to become merely a caretaker who is unable to raise the organization to higher levels of performance in pursuit of important goals. Leaders should remember Lincoln's insight, "A mind stretched by a new idea never returns to its original dimension." Long-range planners can and should stretch the mind of the leader and they should do so regularly.

The long-range planning division with direct access to both the chief executive officer and the other top officials in both the corporate headquarters and the field agencies can be a marvelous clearinghouse for ideas.

One of the great problem areas that all leaders face is a reluctance to develop a mindset which requires spending considerable time planning for a period beyond the leader's expected tenure. This is a particular problem in federal and state government wherein many leaders expect to retain their positions for no more than four years. These restricted time horizons, which are so prevalent in government, are a great detriment to a long-range planning process which should impact on day-to-day decisions.

A major goal of a planning system is to encourage creativity and innovation throughout the organization. Many leaders give lip service to innovation while, at the same time, they fail to create either the climate or the organizational structure to encourage innovation. A leader should periodically examine the quality, quantity, and velocity of innovation within his organization. He should ask how each new idea furthers the mission of the organization. He should be open to new ideas while being sensitive to the turbulence that the implementation of new ideas can often cause in the organization.

A leader should look for ways to increase the velocity of innovation. Many leaders tolerate organizational structures which make the movement of new ideas from originator to key decisionmakers both slow and difficult. Many large organizations are like a long corridor with dozens of doors in a row. If any of the doors is locked, the idea dies. The leader must not only reduce the number of doors, he must also ensure that many people have keys to the doors that remain. The velocity of innovation has two components: the speed and ease by which new ideas can reach the top-level leaders, and the speed and ease of the process whereby the new idea is implemented throughout the organization. Leaders should periodically measure these two aspects of the velocity of innovation; auditors and inspection teams can assist them in this assessment.

The Model Installation Program of the Department of Defense provides a useful example of both innovation and organizational autonomy that is worth examining. The program, which, so far, has been a great success, gives the post or base commander the opportunity to make decisions on his own in order to operate more efficiently and effectively. He is able to keep the money he saves and use it largely as he chooses to improve the operation of his post or base. In the past, such savings were returned to the Federal Treasury. This arrangement provided little incentive to base or post officials to actively seek improvements. The Model Installation Program has many more people actively looking for efficiencies in order to generate funds for badly needed improvements. The substance and velocity of innovation has decidedly improved as a result of this imaginative DOD program. A similar program could have wide applicability in the business world.

Some planning is good; some is bad. There is, however, an unfortunate tendency in this country for many individuals in business and in government to be skeptical of long-range planning. The many failures in the Soviet Union and eastern Europe that seem to be a direct result of poor long-range planning often are cited as examples of why planning is a mistake. It is certainly clear that the ideologically-based planning systems in the totalitarian socialist states have been colossal failures, but these failures should not discourage leaders in democratic states from doing long-range planning. All planning systems can become too rigid and out of touch with reality, but a leader who is a flexible planner and who has a vision based on careful thought and research can lead the organization to new heights of performance and effectiveness. Conversely, a leader who, for ideological (or any other) reasons, rejects planning, misses opportunities. A combination of good systematic planning and flexible "ad-hocracy" can lead to extraordinary results.

16/LEADING INTERNATIONAL ORGANIZATIONS:
dealing with cultural complexities and national antagonisms

LEADERSHIP OF INTERnational organizations is a particularly demanding responsibility since the leader should understand and be sensitive to cultural differences, national biases, antagonisms between and among national groups, unusual administrative and bureaucratic processes, and so forth. When an individual is going to move into a new situation involving the supervision of people from a number of nations, it is useful to do some background reading on each of those nations. For example, books by authors like Samson on England, Barzini on Italy, and Reischauer on Japan are available. Individuals from the various nations are enormously complimented when their boss is able to speak knowledgeably about their history and their traditions; the earlier the reading is done, the better.

In every international organization there will always be some cross-national antagonisms with which the leader must deal. In my two years' experience with individuals from five nations (Great Britain, Germany, Belgium, the Netherlands, and the United States), I found that severe cross-national antagonisms existed. For instance, a few weeks after I moved into the organization, I asked a Dutch lieutenant colonel if he spelled his first name (Frans) with an "S" or a "Z." With considerable anger, he replied that the Germans spelled it with a "Z."

If I had done my research, I would not have asked the question, for I would have known not only the answer, but also the Dutch-German sensitivities. Another example of the manifestation of this antagonism was my German boss who asked me to act as the disciplinarian for any Dutch or Belgian officer who needed counselling. As the German general pointed out to me, "Everyone likes Americans, but some people don't like Germans."

In many cases, there are work-ethic differentials between and among the nations in international organizations. These differences cause morale problems on both sides. Individuals from nations that are accustomed to working short hours and taking long lunch breaks tend to be critical of those who work longer and harder, and vice versa. It is important for the leader to establish a standard for work hours and ensure that the standard is followed. Generally, the standard should be a compromise between the various extremes. Americans tend to work long hours and to be very concerned about "close of business" deadlines and fast responses to messages and taskings. In many cases, when working in international organizations which use English as the official language, Americans must learn to be more patient and give individuals more time to write papers and coordinate issues, particularly if there are a significant number of staff people who lack competency in the English language.

Language difficulties are very common in international organizations. As a result, the nations that speak and write the language of the organization have both a great advantage and a great burden. If English is the language of the organization, as is commonly the case, then the British, the Americans, the Canadians, and other English speakers (the Germans, Dutch, and Scandinavians also tend to be quite proficient in English) will be expected to do most of the work: the writing, the speaking, and the briefing. On the other hand, the leader must ensure that individuals who do not speak and write English as well are not removed from the decisionmaking process and are not neglected in staff activities. This is a very delicate issue. For instance, if they are given only the easy or noncontroversial actions, the leader will soon face a morale problem because those individuals will feel they are being cut out of the important issues and actions.

The leader also must deal with differentials in pay and allowances. There may be civil servants and military officers working side by side with the same ranks or grade levels but with major pay differentials (as much as 100 percent). There is very little that the leader can do about this, but as activities are planned that require individuals to commit their personal funds (parties, receptions, picnics), the leader must be very sensitive to the fact that some people are not as well paid as others.

Within every international organization, there will be nations that are large, rich, and powerful and others that are smaller, poorer, and less powerful. The small nation syndrome must be understood by the leader. Representatives from small nations must be treated with equal care and substantive meetings should include representatives from all nations, even though the issue may have very little to do with one or two of the smaller nations. These nations deserve "a seat at the table," and the leader must ensure that they always have one, for each individual represents a sovereign state despite differences in size or power.

In international military organizations the leader also may have to deal with issues and problems concerning military unions. In certain countries in Europe, military unions are so strong that whenever overtime is demanded, as a result of alerts or exercises, the soldiers must be given compensatory time in the next week or two. These union factors must be weighed carefully to ensure that good training is accomplished while maintaining alert levels and readiness.

A related problem is dealing with military conscripts in many parts of the world. Because the

United States has not had the draft in many years, some Americans have forgotten some of the constraints that a military, based on conscription, imposes on operational readiness, training, and security clearances. If the length of the conscript's service is only 15 months, as it is in many countries, the conscripts are of very little value in many headquarters assignments because they have not been in the military long enough to be able to qualify for higher-level security clearances. In the field, the operational units suffer, because about the time the conscript is fully trained, he leaves military service. Some units are unable to reach high levels of operational readiness and maintain these levels because of rapid turnover of personnel. Such operational units spend the great majority of their time in fairly basic unit training.

In many international organizations there tends to be a "lowest common denominator" phenomenon in evidence. If some nations do not have experience in computers, sophisticated technology, and such, the headquarters tends to be deficient in these areas. It is the responsibility of the leader to try to lift the organization above this lowest common denominator level and bring these countries along within available funding and manpower constraints. In many international organizations, the leader also will have to deal with perquisite differentials. While a Belgian colonel may have his own staff car driver, gardener, and cook, a German brigadier general and an American major general may have none of these. Such differentials can become very important to certain key individuals and may require action on the part of the leader. It is important for the leader to try to compensate in these areas, if possible.

Americans often become "bulls in china shops" when they join an international organization, staff agency, or military unit. The "American way" of dealing with problems sometimes fails in the international milieu. It is particularly important for American leaders of international organizations to be sensitive to national concerns and to listen carefully to their advisors from other nations.

The transition process is important as well when you are about to take over an international organization. You should ensure that the initial briefings are given, to a large extent, by individuals from nations other than your own. Your outer office should include secretaries, executive assistants, protocol officials, and public affairs and community relations specialists from the various nations of the international organization.

In the course of day-to-day business, leaders of large international organizations should spend the great majority of their time with officials from other nations rather than with colleagues from their own nation. This approach is important from the point of view of both substance and perception.

17/ORGANIZING PRIORITIES:
the mission, the mission, the mission

THERE IS A SAYING IN real estate that there are three very important considerations when buying property: location, location, and location. The same can be said about leading a large organization in the sense that a leader must always remember the vital importance of the mission. If the leader is diverted into spending too much time on peripheral issues, the mission will suffer.

There seems to be an insidious tendency in large organizations for leaders' attention to be diverted by the unorganized and unprioritized demands of their schedule, their "in-box," or their telephone calls. Only the most disciplined of leaders gain and maintain control of their schedules; and,

131

even then, leaders must be able and willing to change as circumstances dictate. One of the best examples of the need to be flexible occurred several years ago when an Air Force commander's wing in Europe was undergoing a major "no-notice" operational readiness inspection by higher headquarters. (This is the only time in the entire year when the 4000-person wing has the opportunity to demonstrate to a large team of inspectors its ability to conduct its combat missions.) Instead of being in the command post taking care of the myriad decisions and problems that take place during the loadout of nuclear weapons, the commander was downtown making a speech to some local leaders in the automobile business. He did not adjust his schedule to the situation. He forgot that the mission must come first.

One technique that a leader can use when moving into a new job is to write a personal philosophy letter stressing the importance of the mission and the leader's personal commitment to keeping the mission as the top priority for the organization. Of course, a leader should not only write and speak about the importance of the mission; there must be personal involvement. If a leader is a president or dean of a college or university, that leader also should teach, not only to demonstrate a personal commitment to the goals of the institution, but to have direct interface with the students, staff, and faculty. Teaching is a good way to maintain an awareness of the bureaucratic and administrative problems that the faculty is facing relating to course preparation, syllabus development, printing plant capabilities, and problems that arise for teachers with publishers and guest speakers. If the leader runs a business, there should be a good deal of time spent on the shop floor and even working on the production line, if feasible. A commander of a flying unit should fly the unit aircraft often to remain alert to the operational problems and to become identified by the entire organization as someone who fully grasps the essence of the operational mission. If individuals in an organization wear a large number of different uniforms, the leader might consider wearing those various uniforms in rough proportion to the number of people who wear them. For instance, if 60 percent of the people wear a work or fatigue uniform, 30 percent wear a business suit or service dress uniform, and 10 percent wear flying suits, the leader should wear each uniform in the same proportions, when practicable. If people have to take physical fitness tests periodically, the leader should not only take the tests, but take them with a number of units so that the people can see a personal commitment to maintaining the proper standards of physical conditioning. If some people must pull 24-hour alert duty, the leader should also do so on occasion, if at all possible. Above all, a leader should conserve the organizational energy of the unit and do his very best to ensure that there is no organizational and individual time spent doing work with the sole purpose of making the leader look good, covering up mistakes, or otherwise detracting from mission accomplishment.

One of the paramount requirements of leading large organizations is the need for the leader to joust constantly with the bureaucracy in order to ensure that the organization does not become complacent, stagnant, obsolete, or overly rigid in facing new challenges and opportunities. The problem of institutional rigidity is much greater than just the proclivity of large organizations to be conservative. With less than 20 percent of all professionals within large organizations being "innovators" it is not just organizational conservatism but also individual conservatism—especially in the middle levels of the bureaucracy—that can lead to policy rigidity. Many individuals tend to be more interested in survival, in staying out of trouble, in avoiding extra work, or in being promoted than in carrying out the mission in as effective a way as possible.

Unfortunately, even strong innovators often hide their ideas in the bottom drawer of their desks until the organizational climate is just right for them to surface. This provides a challenge for a leader that is significant but not insurmountable. A climate of trust that helps the innovators come out of their shells can help create an atmosphere of excitement and creativity that can have a major impact on the future of the organization. George Marshall and Hap Arnold are two individuals who provided the climate for the creativity that led to some exciting and important results.

George Marshall's commitment to planning, his knowledge of where the truly talented and innovative young professionals were, and his willingness to hire, nurture, and reward them, all played a vital role in the planning that was done just prior to World War II which led to the success of the Army and the Army Air Corps. Marshall's commitment to creativity played an important role in the establishment of a separate Air Force, the development of the Marshall Plan, and the significant long-range planning efforts in the War Department in the early 1940s, the State Department in the late 1940s, and the Department of Defense in the early 1950s. George Marshall provides a very useful model for an aspiring leader. As both a military and civilian government leader, he was absolutely superb—without peer in his time—in creating an atmosphere of high integrity, trust, creativity, and a sense of mission in all the organizations he led: the US Army, the Department of State, and the Department of Defense.

Hap Arnold also had a strong commitment to planning and innovation. By the summer of 1943, he had created a post-war planning division which focused its full attention on the challenges and opportunities of the post-war world. He also created the RAND Corporation shortly after World War II. This was an important and innovative step. RAND soon become a model of a productive research agency where high quality, policy-relevant, and, most importantly, interdisciplinary research could be accomplished. The creation of RAND and its impact on planning and policy making in the Air Force is historically unique. It set the pattern for many similar research groups which directly support governmental organizations or institutions.

Career patterns within most large governmental organizations may encourage dilettantism as individuals on the way to the top move rapidly from one job to the next. Within the last 20 years it has become a complimentary phrase in government, as well as in many business organizations, for someone to ask, "Can't you hold a job?" What this often means is that some individuals are so bright and successful that they are being moved onward and upward with great rapidity. However, when these individuals reach high-level leadership positions, they have become so accustomed to holding jobs for only one or two years that they often fail to dig deeply into organizational issues, problems, programs, and opportunities. As a result, they sometimes fail as leaders. Their time horizons have been habitually short, and their proclivities toward dilettantism are exacerbated by rapidly changing career patterns.

When you are selected to lead a large organization, this new challenge should be approached with a very different mindset than when selected for a normal staff or lower level leadership position. You must realize that most of your subordinates want you to succeed, but a few will want you to fail. Most will carry out your guidance with enthusiasm and skill. Conversely, some will work against this guidance in hopes of undercutting your initiatives. In all large organizations, there will be individuals who tend to resist new initiatives unless they are their own ideas. The leader should, therefore, strive to capture the imagination and support of subordinates by letting them come up with new ideas. It is a wise leader, indeed, who listens carefully to subordinates and helps to turn their best ideas into organizational initiatives. Patience can pay off handsomely.

Great leaders exercise self-abnegation regularly and often; it is the sign of a great leader never to take credit for the success of the organization. Self-aggrandizement is a counterproductive quality in a leader. The leader who gets up in front of any group and states that the organization that he or she has led for the last two years was initially in terrible shape, but is in wonderful shape today, reveals a great deal. An objective observer would conclude that the organization was probably not as bad as this leader says it was two years ago, and not as good as proclaimed today. The truly mature leader will most likely say that the organization was in fine shape on arrival and any improvements that have taken place are the result of the talents and hard work of subordinates.

It is wise for a leader of a large organization to consider the point that Henry Kissinger made many years ago in his book, *The Necessity for Choice*, "One of the paradoxes of an increasingly specialized, bureaucratized society is that the qualities required in the rise to eminence are less and less the qualities required once eminence is reached." Individuals who move into leadership jobs, who do not take a very hard look at themselves and who do not think about the differences between leading small organizations and large organizations, or between being a staff person and the leader, may be unable to provide the mature leadership required. To quote David Ogilvie, "The recipe for success is first, making a reputation for creative genius; second, surround yourself with partners who are better than you are; third, leave them to get on with it."

137

A question that a leader should often ask subordinates is, "How can I help you, and how can I make your job easier?" A related question is, "What am I doing that is making your job difficult and what is it about my style or my decisions that really bother you?" If a leader doesn't ask these kinds of questions periodically, the leader is liable to become part of the problem rather than part of the solution. You may think you are doing a great job, while, in fact, other people may be spending a great deal of their time picking up after you or trying to reduce the impact of the mistakes that you are making.

A leader of a large organization should not only know what is happening within the organization and have solid operational and technical competence, but also should avoid spending a great deal of time in the details of the decision. Someone once suggested that one of our recent presidents didn't look at the forest, he didn't look at the trees, but he spent all his time looking at the leaves on the trees. This tendency toward micromanagement should be scrupulously avoided.

A leader must be loyal to the boss, the mission, the people, the organization, the nation and, in some cases, to a supranational or international organization such as NATO, the Organization of American States, or the United Nations. Keeping these loyalties in proper perspective is a very important aspect of mature leadership. Almost everyone has a boss, and although leaders of large organizations have a great deal of autonomy, both in policymaking and in geographic span, they still must answer to someone, whether it be their commander, a board of directors, the stockholders, the US Congress, or the American people. Elbert Hubbard's remarks ring true on the issue of loyalty. He said, "Remember this. If you work for a man, in heaven's name, work for him. If he pays you wages which supply you bread and butter, work for him; speak well of him; stand by him and stand by the institution he represents. If put to a pinch, an ounce of loyalty is worth a pound of cleverness. If you must vilify, condemn and eternally disparage—resign your position, and when you are on the outside, damn to your heart's content, but as long as you are part of the institution do not condemn it."

There is a fundamental paradox in leading large organizations that all leaders must understand and grapple with as best they can. The bigger the organization, the more trust is required, yet the harder it is to engender and reinforce trust. Leaders must not only trust subordinates, they must believe in their competence, perhaps more so than these subordinates believe in themselves.

Keeping an eye on the goals and making sure that priorities stay in order are not always easy tasks for a leader. For those in public service, the West Point motto is a useful guide: "Duty, Honor, Country." A public servant must be willing to resign if these fundamental principles cannot be upheld.

18/TAKING CARE OF YOUR PEOPLE:
sponsorship, not cronyism

A VITAL ROLE FOR A leader is that of ensuring that subordinates are properly rewarded, promoted, and moved on to subsequent and more senior assignments in a deliberate and thoughtful way. A leader should identify the very best and help them get their next higher jobs within the organization or in other related organizations. The leader should monitor their careers and help them achieve their full potential.

On the other hand, the leader should be very careful not to fall into the trap of cronyism. Pushing "his boys" can often cause great morale problems within the organization. Practicing cronyism also can often hurt people by trying to help them; a leader who pushes a person into a big job before he or she is capable of handling that job, or forces a protégé on a subordinate leader, often does the protégé a great disservice. In the second example, if the subordinate leader really does not want the individual, it is very likely that the individual's career, in the longer term, will be hurt working for that subordinate leader.

A related problem to dealing with cronyism is handling sycophancy. Unfortunately, in all large organizations there are individuals who are very skillful in pleasing the boss by bearing good news and by playing on the boss's ego. These individuals normally can be identified as those who are always looking for ways to make the boss happy, who worry about getting a lot of "face time" with the boss and who are personally ambitious. There is a direct relationship between cronyism and sychophancy. Leaders must be sensitive to this significant problem area in large organizations.

A leader also should pay particular attention to the "late bloomer." Within every organization, there are people of enormous talent who have matured later in life than their contemporaries. The late bloomer needs particular attention since personnel managers generally tend to overlook their career potential because this potential was not evident early.

A number of dysfunctional qualities sometimes develop in very talented people. The first dysfunctional quality is arrogance; no matter how talented an individual may be, if very arrogant this person will be unlikely to succeed, over the long term, as a leader. Additionally, many individuals who exhibit potential early in their career do not live up to expectations. Leaders who are sponsoring individuals should periodically look at them with a critical eye to be sure that they are not pushing them beyond their capabilities. A general rule of thumb worth considering when you identify individuals with great talent and potential is the "one-push" rule. Give these individuals one strong upward push and then leave them alone. If the talent and potential are truly outstanding, those individuals will keep moving upward with no additional help from you. For those who have reached their ultimate level of potential and competence, further sponsorship to higher positions is a mistake.

George Marshall probably provides the best model in the area of constructive sponsorship. He had carefully identified people of great talent and potential during the first 35 years of his Army career. When he was selected by President Roosevelt to be the Chief of Staff of the Army in the late 1930s, he had a carefully comprised list of outstanding people in the Army and Army Air Corps. He used this list to select individuals for key staff and command positions in the immediate pre-war period. When war broke out, he used this list extensively to pick the top wartime leaders. To a very large extent the US military did extremely well in World War II because of General Marshall's careful sponsorship of people of talent, character, and leadership potential.

On the other hand, leaders should not bring a substantial number of former colleagues with them when they move to new positions. A leader who drags a large coterie of "the old gang" to the new job is likely to undermine the morale of the new organization. It also will be difficult to develop good rapport with new subordinates and communication

143

channels will be harder to establish. In addition, a leader will gain more credibility as a person of self-confidence and independent thought if that leader does not rely on a group of old cronies.

Finally, leaders of large organizations should provide guidance to subordinate leaders and personnel managers concerning the criteria for promotion. The promotion system must be fair and perceived to be so. Members of promotion panels or boards should be selected very carefully by the leader; the leader should give specific written guidance to each board. And the leader should meet privately with the head of the promotion board prior to the time that it meets. After the board completes its work, the head should report back to the leader and state specifically where the board was unable to fully carry out its guidance. Appendix A includes a useful checklist for promotion boards. It is a modified version of a checklist that was generously provided to me by the Commandant of the United States Coast Guard, Admiral J.S. Gracey.

19/TEACHING:
leadership essential

GOOD LEADERS TEND TO be good teachers and use various means to exercise "teachership" responsibility. Staff meetings, for instance, are marvelous teaching opportunities, as are welcoming briefings for new people in the organization, speaking engagements at professional schools, and, of course, teaching in one-on-one situations.

One useful technique is to make a videotape where the leader is introduced and then discusses the history of the organization, states the philosophy, goals and priorities, and speaks about the importance of the mission and the important role of all the people. This tape has many uses. It can be shown to new employees, visitors, the members of the media, etc. If resources permit, the videotape should be done professionally; it should be short (10 to 15 minutes), and it should be updated every year or two.

Part of teachership is the planting of good ideas into the minds of subordinates in such subtle ways that they soon feel these ideas are their own. A good leader probably has a lot of good ideas, but he will be a more effective leader if new ideas are perceived as and credited with having come from others within the organization. If those in an organization feel that it has reached high levels of excellence on its own without the direction of its leaders, when, in fact, many of the ideas that were implemented came from the leader, the leader has been very successful indeed. A leader should take silent satisfaction when such ideas are captured by others. It is a wise leader who takes the attitude of first grade teachers, who, at the end of the year, receive no thanks from the children but know they have educated them well in their preparation for the next level. A good example is Fox Connor who was the great teacher of Eisenhower, Marshall, and others. His teachership was quiet and subtle. He looked for no praise, but received great satisfaction out of the brilliant performance of his students as they led the US Army in World War II and in the post-war era.

A leader should not only be a teacher of subordinate leaders but should also teach them how to be teachers themselves, by establishing personal standards, by being an example which others can emulate, by taking the time to teach, and by teaching systematically and regularly.

Some of the questions a leader might ask people periodically are: What have we learned from this experience? How can we avoid a similar setback (if there has been one) in the future? Could we have handled this problem better if we were organized differently? and, How do we get our people thinking and talking more about goals?

Periodic off-site retreats are excellent teaching opportunities. Leaders of organizations should invite their key subordinates to an area which is geographically removed from the normal work area for a two or three day retreat every year. The atmosphere should be a relaxed one. Attendees should remain on site overnight. Sports should be scheduled in the late afternoons (round robin tennis tournaments, volleyball, or softball work well as sports mixers). Spouses should not be included. Roommates should be paired so that each new individual rooms with a person who has been with the organization for some time. The leader should open the retreat with a general statement of philosophy, goals, priorities, and concerns, and should review the past year by highlighting both the high and low points (a chart showing highs and lows can be helpful in this regard). The leader should emphasize the major upcoming events over the next few months and explain why they are important to the organization. The leader should thank subordinates for their outstanding work and encourage them to seek even higher levels of excellence next year. Initially, the leader also should establish the rules of the game for the retreat such as: all discussions are off the record and everyone should speak with total candor. Questions should be encouraged: What successes have we enjoyed and what have been the secrets to these successes? What is really bothering you about the organization and my leadership style? What opportunities are we missing? What mistakes have we made or are we making? How can we make next year even more productive?

Before going on the retreat it is useful for the leader to send a short questionnaire to all the people who will be attending. The questionnaire should ask: What were the high and low points of the year? What new initiatives do you intend to take next year? Who would be a good speaker from outside our organization for the retreat? and, What topics should we address at the retreat?

A major aspect of teachership is the maintenance of a reading program on the part of the leader. It is often said that the really tough jobs cause people to burn up intellectual capital because they stay so busy that they have little time to read, research, or reflect. Leaders who manage their time well can continue to read and gain insights from the best books and articles in their field.

Leaders should read good history, biographies, and autobiographies, as well as books on management, leadership, strategy, planning, and the long-term future. One of the subjects that should be addressed on every off-site retreat is a list of the best books that the leader and his subordinates have read over the past year. Leaders should have cerebral energy and should demonstrate that energy not only by establishing a systematic reading program for themselves, but also by encouraging their subordinates to read important literature in their fields. Leaders should display in prominent places in their offices books they have read lately. As leaders read new books, these books should replace the ones that have been on the coffee table in the previous weeks. In this way leaders can demonstrate visibly to all subordinates and visitors their commitment to a serious reading program. One useful technique is for the leader to mark each book and to engage the author in a running conversation by making comments in the margin. Another technique is for the leader to mark the book with a "quote-file" notation that the executive secretary can then place in a file for the leader that can be used in speeches, articles, letters. In this way, leaders can ensure that future speeches have lots of fresh material that has been generated through the reading program. Through these techniques, leaders can keep up with their fields, with changing thoughts on leadership and management, and make future speeches at a high level of excellence and relevance.

When leaders go on trips, take vacations, or go home for weekends, they should try to avoid taking the "in-box" home. If leaders manage their time well, they should get to the bottom of the in-box by the end of the week and have time for outside reading on weekends, holidays, and trips.

A wonderful way to establish and maintain a productive reading program is to read, on a weekly basis, a significant number of book reviews. Most professional journals have book review sections. In addition, the *New York Times*, Sunday edition, has a first-rate book review section. A good general rule is: Don't buy a book until you have read at least two book reviews to ensure that reading the book is worth your valuable time.

Leaders who read a book each week are doing a reasonably good job of maintaining cerebral energy and intellectual curiosity. They should mix serious books of non-fiction which relate directly or indirectly to his or her chosen field with "fun" books of fiction, biography, humor, travel, etc.

A useful technique to maximize the value of reading time is to read the first and last chapter of each book. If, after reading the first and last chapters, the leader has not been sufficiently inspired by the author's ideas and insights, reading the rest of the book may be largely a waste of time. In addition to reading on trips, weekends, and vacations, leaders should consider reading early in the morning, prior to going to work. Executives who arrive at work late, by perhaps an hour or so, give their staff a chance to clean up the work of the previous day and to be ready for their queries and demands. A wonderful way to break the habit pattern of a lifetime of coming to work early is to schedule reading time at home prior to departing for work.

Since leaders should be visionaries and planners, they should spend some time reading books about the long-term future. There have been a number of excellent mind-stretching books in recent years that can help leaders ask their planners the right questions. The following is a short list of books in this category: Kahn's *The Coming Boom*; Naisbitt's *Megatrends*; Cetron's *Encounters with the Future*; and Toffler's *The Third Wave*.

If a leader has been a good teacher, the organization will be in stronger shape, and the job for the next leader will be easier. If a leader is spending a great deal of time teaching, and only a modest amount of time problem solving and deciding, the leader probably has the priorities straight.

20/WRAPPING UP

THIS BOOK HAS BEEN designed to give a leader practical thoughts on how to run large organizations. Although there are a number of checklists provided, it is important to emphasize that complete reliance on "checklist" or "cookbook" leadership can be a mistake. Anyone who runs an organization but cannot adapt to the situations not contained in checklists in conducting day-to-day activities is doomed to fail as an enlightened leader. Therefore, readers should accept the ideas, insights, and checklists that are provided with a certain amount of skepticism. Much that happens in big organizations is truly unique; however, the lessons of others may be helpful as a leader struggles with current problems.

It is important for leaders to do their own thinking, to read widely and to talk with and listen to others within and without their own organizations. Leaders should never rely on one key associate or assistant to do their thinking for them. If they do so, in a very real sense they are no longer leaders.

"Before a leader makes a decision, it is useful to ask a few questions. Who is going to be mad? How mad? Who is going to be happy? How happy?" This insight from Paul Appleby is useful, for it highlights the need for a leader to anticipate the reactions of subordinates and others who may be affected by key decisions. Anticipating reactions should not paralyze a leader preparing to make decisions, but considering reactions helps frame the right questions before one makes those leadership decisions.

Leadership is not synonymous with authority. It is, to a very considerable extent, a value which is entrusted to the superior by the subordinate. It embodies an emotional, often spiritual, investment by the subordinate in his superior, a gift of trust. To a great extent, the subordinate defines the conditions under which trust is given. He prescribes those qualities, characteristics, and values his superior must possess in order to be accepted as his leader. It is the wise leader, indeed, who understands and nurtures the relationship between superior and subordinate.

Admiral James Stockdale, who has written powerfully and meaningfully about leadership, has good advice for all of us. He believes that individuals who are not willing to discipline people, who are unwilling to remove people, and who crave to be loved, all tend to be poor leaders. Stockdale states, "Truly, leaders must be willing to stake out territory and declare enemies." As we train and educate leaders, it is more important to teach key people how to deal with failure than how to deal with success. Another insight is found in his book, *A Vietnam Experience*, "Strange as it sounds, great leaders gain authority by giving it away."

It is vitally important that leaders do not let the urgent force out the important in their day-to-day activities. They should spend their talents lavishly rather than hoarding them. Leadership should be a giving rather than a taking experience. The attitude of the leader is important because the posture assumed in day-to-day activities can have a great impact on the morale of an organization. If the leader is a negative person, it is likely that subordinates will adopt a negative disposition. On the other hand, if the leader is cheerful, the cheerfulness will spread throughout the organization. People want to feel good about themselves, their organization, and what they are doing.

Colonel Jack Jacobs, US Army, has pointed out that, "A leader of a large organization may often have to accept rotten circumstances in order to make overall progress. The high-level leader who will accept nothing less than the perfection that can be achieved at great cost will lose everything. This is not to say that standards must be low; on the contrary, it is at the highest levels that high standards originate. But the leader has to have the kind of long-range vision that will overlook short-term setbacks." The leader must understand a truism of large organizations: "The perfect can be the enemy of the good." A leader crosses an important milestone when signing that first imperfect, but wholly adequate, staff paper without editing or changing it personally.

Leadership functions must be shared with "lieutenants." The organization will become healthier as the leader creates more centers of leadership within the organization. Leaders must take particular care in nurturing their relationships with their deputies. The deputy leader must be given authority to make decisions in the absence of the leader and those decisions must be supported enthusiastically by the leader. The deputy should be included in all substantive meetings, discussions, and decisions so that the entire institution understands that the deputy has authority, responsibility, and credibility.

If the leader comes from a specialized area, whether it be marketing, personnel, logistics, engineering, operations, or any other, there must be personal initiative to grow beyond that specialized field. A true leader will always be fundamentally challenged rather than repelled by complexity. Leaders should focus primarily on opportunities, not on problems.

Leaders must be generalists; those who select individuals for leadership positions should pick individuals who have the capacity to grow and to become gifted generalists. If the leader is to ensure organizational creativity and innovation, there must be tolerance for the creative fanatic who, in many cases, is the force behind important innovations. The leader must realize that large and complex organizations often suppress new ideas, new opinions and new alternatives. Leaders must fight against the bureaucratic tendencies to create watered-down compromises that are often less than desirable solutions. There is a sign on a rural road in upstate New York which says, "Choose your rut carefully, you will be in it for the next 25 miles." A leader is someone who identifies the "ruts" within an organization and makes sure that individuals or groups of individuals do not stay in these "ruts" for the next 25 weeks, 25 months, or 25 years.

In every organization, there are many people who are not pulling their share of the load because of their own incompetency, laziness, poor attitudes, psychological difficulties, bad habits, or family problems. It is the role of the leader to deal with these people and either to motivate them, isolate them, or, as a last resort, remove them. One of the frustrating things about dealing with large organizations is the difficulty in removing incompetent individuals. A leader must be very aggressive in this regard; although it might take a great amount of time and effort to deal with incompetents, the effectiveness and morale of the organization depend upon maintaining high standards of competence and integrity. A leader must be willing to establish, maintain, and enforce those standards.

There is no activity in human endeavor that is more fascinating, more challenging, and more rewarding than leading large and complex organizations with an important mission. The leaders who are willing to grow, learn, listen, acknowledge mistakes, teach subordinates, set goals, and maintain high standards are leaders who can help lift an organization to new heights. Tom Cronin challenges each of us when he writes: "Leaders have those indispensable qualities of contagious self-confidence, unwarranted optimism and incurable idealism that allow them to attract and mobilize others to undertake tasks these people dreamed they could not undertake." This is the true task of the leader.

APPENDIX A
checklists for busy leaders

The following checklists are provided to help leaders accomplish several of the important tasks that confront them. Operational checklists can be important in two major areas: in ensuring a task that must be done very quickly is accomplished in proper order, and in ensuring that a vital step or element is not left out. Leadership checklists serve the same basic purposes.

These checklists are not substitutes for judgment, but they can trigger the mind and make the task at hand somewhat easier.

a. transition checklist
b. communications checklist
c. integrity checklist
d. hiring checklist
e. counselling checklist
f. hang-up checklist
g. firing checklist
h. thank you checklist

i. planning checklist
j. divestiture checklist
k. decisionmaking checklist
l. executive skills checklist
m. meeting checklist
n. introspection checklist
o. promotion board checklist
p. "antenna" checklist
q. phrases to avoid checklist
r. congressional visit checklist

a. *transition checklist*   The following are useful questions to ask when you have been selected to assume a leadership position. They are also useful questions for the departing leader to answer for the incoming leader.

- What is the mission?

- What are the organization's
    - —goals?
    - —priorities?
    - —plans?
    - —programs?
    - —budgets?

- What is the size and structure of the organization?

- What means of communications will I have?
    - —newspaper/newsletter
    - —radio
    - —television
    - —staff meetings
    - —commander's calls
    - —formal and informal seminars
    - —social gatherings

- Who reports directly to me?
    - —how many?
    - —why?
    - —why not others?

- Who is my boss?
    - —what is his leadership/management style?
    - —what is his means of communication to me?

- Am I responsible for geographically separated units?
    - —do they report directly to me?
    - —do they report indirectly to me?
- Which organizations, staff agencies and individuals should I visit?
    - —in what order?
    - —how often for subsequent visits?
- What is the standard of integrity?
    - —have there been recent violations of these standards?
    - —how frequent and what was the outcome?
- What are the standards of performance?
    - —how are they measured?
    - —what are the results of recent
        - —outside inspections?
        - —self-inspections?
        - —audits?
        - —staff-assistance visits?
- What documents should I read?
    - —in what order?
    - —is there an annual organizational history? if not, why not?
    - —is there a book of standard operating procedures; organizational regulations?
    - —what are the most important plans?
    - —is there a long-range plan? if not, why not?
- What skeletons are in what closet?
    - —organizational skeletons?
    - —personal skeletons?
- Where are the personnel shortages/weaknesses?

- What is the condition of the industrial plant buildings, unit equipment, etc.?
- What are the major logistics problems?
- What are the toughest problems and issues I should expect to face during the first few months?
- How often do the top leaders and their immediate subordinates go to "off-site" seminars together?

b. *communications checklist*   Many leaders fail to use fully the means of communications that are, or can be, made available to them. This checklist may be helpful to ensure that opportunities are not missed.

- Is there an organization newspaper?
    - —how often is it published?
    - —what is its quality?
    - —does the leader have a space reserved for a weekly/monthly column?
    - —how wide is the readership?
    - —what percentage of the readership actually reads the leader's column?
    - —is there a feedback channel?
        - —letters to the editor?
        - —letters to the commander?
        - —action line?
- Does the leader have regular access to:
    - —radio?
    - —television?
    - —closed circuit television?
- Are there regular staff meetings?
    - —are minutes taken, published and circulated?
    - —do participants feel free to raise issues?
- Are there work unit meetings or commander's calls?
- Is there a public affairs office?
    - —does the public affairs officer report directly to you? if not, why not?
    - —what are the public affairs officer's ideas on how best to communicate to the troops?

- Are subordinate organizations being publicly praised and thanked? In what ways and through what means?
- Is there a movie or videotape that explains the organization to new people, visitors, guests, families, community leaders, etc.? If not, why not?

c. *integrity checklist* There are certain areas in organizations where integrity is tested often. It is important for the leader periodically to check these areas to ensure that high standards of integrity are being maintained:

- the inspection system
- the training system
- the management control system
- the reporting system
- the testing system
- congressional testimony
- submission of programs and budgets
- training competitions
- records within the personnel system

d. *hiring checklist*   When hiring a subordinate, the interview is recommended in order for the leader to get a "feel" for the individual and for the "chemistry" between the leader and the prospective subordinate. If a face-to-face interview is not possible, an interview by telephone can be an acceptable substitute. When checking the individual out with other individuals, some of these questions can also be useful.

- Do you want the job? Why?
- What talents, qualities and strengths would you bring to this job?
- What are your weaknesses?
- How long would you like to hold this job?
- What is your leadership/management style?
- If I asked a subordinate of yours to describe you and your leadership style, what would be the response?
- If you are not selected, whom would you recommend for this job?
- What are the best books you have read in the last few years? What insights did they provide you?
- What are your long-term personal goals?
- Do you expect to be promoted soon?
- Are there any "skeletons in your closet"?
- Whom in your present organization do you admire the most and why?
- What is the standard of integrity in your present organization?
- Are you considering any other positions?

- If I select you for this job, would you take it as your first choice over other positions you are considering?
- Are you approaching a retirement decision soon?
- How many people have you led or supervised in your career?
- Have you ever fired anyone? Have you ever been fired?
- What experience do you have with
  —operations?
  —planning?
  —finance/marketing?
  —research and development?
  —manpower and personnel?
  —computer systems?
- Have you had any setbacks in your career?
  —if so, what were the most significant lessons learned from the setbacks?
  —what organizational setbacks have you observed at first hand?
- What is the toughest problem you have ever faced in your professional career? How have you handled it?

e. *counselling checklist*   This checklist can be a helpful guide when you have one-on-one sessions with your subordinates. Any checklist used in this regard should be committed to memory so that the one-on-one session does not become too formal or structured. Prior to your semi-annual series of one-on-one sessions, you may wish to circulate a list of questions along the general lines of this checklist to give your subordinates an idea of the questions you are going to ask and the points you are going to cover.

- What aspects of this organization do you like the most?

- What areas around here bother you the most?

- What are your ideas for improving this organization?

- What organizations, programs, doctrines, tactics, weapons systems, etc., should we divest ourselves of, and on what kind of schedule (now, next year, five years from now, etc.)?

- In your judgment, who are the most innovative, helpful, and cooperative people in this organization?

- What are your personal goals while you are in this organization?

- Where and to what job would you like to go next; why and when?

- What do you consider to be your most significant weaknesses?

- What self-improvement programs do you have underway?

167

- What do you think your chances are for promotion to the next rank or position, and in what time frame?
- What bothers you the most about my decisions and my leadership style?
- What three things cause you to waste your time the most?
- Is there anything I am doing that wastes your time?
- What are the goals you have established for your organization?
- Please evaluate the performance of the organization, unit or group that you led over the past year (or in the period since we last had a one-on-one session). Please outline the high and low points of the period.

f. *hang-up checklist* All leaders should know their "hang-ups" and articulate them to their subordinates when they assume their leadership position and periodically thereafter. Since a hang-up checklist is very much a personal statement of the leader's biases, concerns, idiosyncrasies, etc., each leader must prepare his or her own. The following is a proposed hang-up checklist. It is illustrative only and should be used as a very general guide.

- Low levels of integrity
- Careerism/hyperambition
- Lack of style
- Missing suspenses
- Being used
- Rumormongering
- Parochialism
- Retirement on the job
- Dilettantism
- Not telling the full story
- Authoritarianism

g. *firing checklist* This difficult duty can become somewhat easier if it is accomplished systematically and if the leader can maintain a sense of concern and empathy while, at the same time, sticking with the decision to remove the individual. During the one-on-one session, the individual should be given adequate time to vent displeasure or disagreement with the decision. The leader can gain useful insights about problems within the organization from passive listening during this session.

- Outline reasons for the decision:
    - —loss of confidence in subordinate's abilities
    - —incompetence
        - —as a supervisor/leader/manager
        - —as a writer
        - —as a teacher
    - —lack of ability to meet deadlines
    - —lack of integrity
    - —poor attitude
    - —chronic absenteeism
    - —inability to get along with boss/peers/subordinates
- Ask individual what he or she might want to do next and how you can help.
- Ask individual what lessons can be drawn from this setback.
- Ask individual if there are any things about the organization that you should know.

h. *thank you checklist*   These are a few ways to thank the folks who do so much to make your organization thrive.

Many thanks for:

- your contribution to the mission
- your integrity
- making my job easy
- adding elegance and style to our organization
- caring
- your commitment to excellence
- your marvelous attitude
- your willingness to take on the tough jobs
- your willingness to work cooperatively with people
- your willingness to tell it like it is
- your willingness to take risks
- your courage
- your self-sacrifice
- your creativity
- your courtesy
- your sincerity
- your love
- your sensitivity
- setting and maintaining high standards
- meeting our goals
- exceeding our goals
- your ideas
- your vision
- your tolerance
- your leadership

- your teachership
- your contributions
- your dedication
- your professionalism
- your receptivity to ideas
- your sound advice
- your common sense
- your responsiveness
- your loyalty
- your honesty
- your willingness to criticize constructively
- your ability to rise above parochialism
- your cerebral energy
- your ability to conceptualize
- your style
- your maturity
- your lack of pettiness

i. *planning checklist*   A major responsibility for a leader is to establish a strategic vision for the organization. A plans office and an institutionalized planning system can be helpful in this regard. Some useful questions about planning follow:

- What are your organization's plans?
- How large is the planning staff?
- Do they report directly to you? If not, why not?
- Is there a long-range plan?
    - —how is it used and by whom?
    - —if not, what is the strategic vision of your organization?
- Does your planning system include:
    - —manpower and personnel planning?
    - —resource planning?
    - —facility/construction planning?
    - —logistics planning?
    - —operational planning?
    - —contingency planning?
    - —opportunity planning?
    - —economic planning?
    - —investment planning?
- What is the staff relationship between the chief planner and
    - —the chief of personnel?
    - —the chief of manpower?
    - —the chief of logistics?
    - —the chief of finance?
    - —the chief of operations?
    - —the field organizations?
- What kind of divestiture is taking place?

- What major innovations are underway in your organization?
- How often is there a planning/innovation off-site seminar?
- Are there regular, scheduled meetings between you and your long-range planners? Do these meetings lead to any decisions?

j. *divestiture checklist*

- What short-term and long-term impact will this divestiture opportunity have on the mission of the organization? Will the short-term disadvantages be outweighed by the long-term advantages?

- What are the principal advantages of this divestiture opportunity?

- What are the principal disadvantages of this divestiture opportunity?

- How much money, manpower, and other resources will be saved as a result of this divestiture? How easy will it be to transfer these resources into more productive areas?

- What impact will this divestiture have on the overall philosophy, priorities, and goals of this organization?

- Will the goals, priorities, and philosophy of the organization have to be changed as a result of this divestiture?

- Do I have the authority to make this decision myself?

- With whom should I consult before I make my decision?

- Should I call in an outside consultant to get a disinterested opinion on the wisdom of this divestiture proposal?

- What are the alternative means by which this divestiture can be implemented? Which is the best scheme?

- Who will lose their jobs and how involved should I be in counselling them and finding them attractive new job opportunities?

- Does this divestiture provide opportunities to do other important things, such as reorganization, removing incompetent employees, etc.?

- What are the various ways that resources which are saved can be applied to other areas within the organization? Which is the best way?

- How will this divestiture be perceived by the employees throughout the organization? Will it be interpreted as being the first of a number of divestiture steps which may threaten many jobs throughout the organization?

- How should the decision be announced? Should I do it myself?

k. *decisionmaking checklist*

- Is the coordination completed?
- Have all key line and staff agencies had the opportunity to comment, criticize, or express their nonconcurrence on the options and recommendations?
- Do I have the authority to make this decision? If not, who does?
- Is this the right time to decide?
- Would postponing the decision help or hurt the mission of the organization?
- What will be the general reaction throughout my organization?
  —will it help or hurt morale?
  —will it undermine my legitimacy as the leader?
  —will it significantly enhance output or mission accomplishment?
- Has informal coordination with outside organizations taken place already? If not, should I telephone some key people to make sure that my decision doesn't receive too much negative reaction and criticism?
- How should this decision be announced?
  —at a press conference?
  —at a staff meeting?
  —by a decision letter?
  —by telephone calls to superiors and key subordinates?
- Does the statement announcing the decision include a complete rationale for the decision?

- Does this decision conform to my long-range plan?
- Is it faithful to my goals and priorities?
- Is it consistent with my previous decisions?
- If I am about ready to launch off in a new direction, do I need to change my long-range plan, my goals, or my priorities?

1. *executive skills checklist*

- Are you skilled in giving dictation?
  - —to your secretary?
  - —to a dictaphone?
- Are you a speed reader? If not, do you plan to take a course in speed reading soon?
- Who arranges your schedule?
  - —have you provided definitive guidelines on your schedule to your executive secretary or to your administrative assistant?
  - —does your daily schedule have more than one event per hour? If so, are you over-scheduled?
  - —do you have time to think, to write, to plan, to be introspective?
- In your yearly calendar, when do you plan to have your off-site seminar with key subordinates?
  - —when do you plan to schedule your one-on-one sessions with key subordinates?
  - —on what schedule do you plan to visit your geographically-separated field organizations?
  - —what is your vacation schedule?
- When was the last time you rewrote your philosophy letter?
- How current is your long-range plan?
  - —how often are you meeting with the long-range planning division?
  - —does your long-range planning division serve as a clearinghouse for new ideas and innovations?

- What is the quality, timing, and effectiveness of your organizational newspaper, magazine, or newsletter?
    —what kind of feedback mechanisms are available to measure its impact?
    —does it serve the mission directly, indirectly, or both?
    —what percentage of your subordinates read it?
- Who in your organization is totally frank with you?
    —what are the subordinates saying about you over a cup of coffee or at the bar?
    —which subordinates are sychophants?
- What are your major weaknesses as a leader? What are you doing to improve these weak areas?
- Are you perceived as:
    —out of touch?
    —past your prime?
    —authoritarian?
    —non-decisive?
    —a captive of your staff?
    —arrogant?
    —intense?
    —biased?
    —self-righteous?
    —lazy?
    —a micromanager?
    —an alcoholic?
    —lacking in style?
    —preoccupied?
    —aloof?
    —a philanderer?

- What are the means by which new ideas bubble up to the top in your organization?
- How many new ideas have been implemented in the past year?
- What legacy do you wish to leave behind you?
- Which subordinates are capable of replacing you?

m. *meeting checklist*

- What is the purpose of the meeting? What is the agenda?
- Who will be in attendance?
  - —have all the appropriate agencies, staff groups, field organizations, nations, etc. been invited?
  - —is the chief lawyer in attendance or properly represented?
- How much time is allocated for the meeting?
  - —do any key players have to leave early? if so, who? should the agenda be adjusted accordingly?
  - —what plan do you have to keep the meeting on track?
- Who will be the recorder for the meeting?
  - —will there be minutes?
  - —will action items be committed to writing after the meeting?
- Are there presentations to be made?
  - —if so, by whom?
  - —are there time limits placed on each presentation?
  - —will there be enough time for adequate discussion?
- Will decisions be taken during the meeting?
  - —if so, will you announce them at the end?
  - —if not, should you announce when and how decisions will be taken?

- What is your meeting strategy?
    - —who are the main antagonists?
    - —is compromise possible? is compromise wise? will compromise lead to a watered-down solution?
- Who will be responsible for implementation of decisions?
- Will additional meetings be needed?
    - —should these meetings be announced prior to the end of this meeting?
    - —if not, will you announce that this is the final meeting on this subject?
- If key players cannot attend, can they be hooked up through a teleconference system or some other means?
- Do you have an overall policy on length of meetings, number of presentations, and length of presentations?
    - —in this meeting, do you intend to hold to these constraints?
    - —if not, do you intend to announce your position at the start of the meeting?
- Do you intend to run the meeting yourself or to allow someone else to chair the meeting?

n. *introspection checklist*

- Do you plan your weekly and monthly schedule carefully? Do you stick to it fairly closely? Does your executive secretary help you maintain your schedule?

- Have you established organizational priorities? Do you and your subordinates stick to these priorities consistently?

- How reliable are you? How many meetings, speeches, trips, social engagements, professional commitments, etc. have you cancelled during the past month?

- Who tells you all the news—good and bad?

- How long are your meetings?

- How well do you listen? Do you spend at least 75 percent of your time listening when you interact with others?

- Do people fear you, distrust you, like you, respect you, love you? How courteous are you?

- What is your body language like?

- Are you considered a communicator?

- Are you considered a disciplinarian?

- Do you enjoy your job?

- Are you flexible?

- Do you maintain physical and intellectual fitness?

- Are you a deflector of pressure from above or a magnifier of that pressure?

- Are you tuned in or out of touch?

- Are you a delegator?

- Are you a non-drinker, a drinker, an alcoholic?
- Are you an optimist or a pessimist?
- Are you religious? What are your ethics and values?
- Are you a writer?
- Are you ambitious?
- Are you secure or insecure?
- Are you a philanderer?
- What is your integrity level?
- Are you an intense individual or are you relaxed?
- Are you decisive or are you a "decision ducker"?
- How conceptual are you?

o. *promotion board checklist* This checklist was created by Admiral J.S. Gracey, the Commandant of the Coast Guard. He has generously permitted its use in the classroom and in this book.

TO PROMOTION BOARD MEMBERS: IN SELECTING FUTURE LEADERS, ASK YOURSELF THE FOLLOWING QUESTIONS ABOUT EACH PERSON.

IS THIS PERSON:

- a self starter?
- willing to go out on a limb?
- willing to walk the extra mile?
- courteous and considerate, especially to/of juniors?
- a professional?
- biased in any way?
- afraid of making a mistake?
- socially active and adept? Is his/her spouse?
- strong only in his/her own "specialty," or can he/she contribute in the whole range of activities of the firm, service, or agency?
- willing to try new things, even at some risk?
- practical and realistic?
- warm and personable?
- capable of being a maverick? Does he/she always insist on being a maverick?
- perceptive?
- innovative?

DOES THIS PERSON:

- tell me what he/she thinks, not tell me what he/she thinks I want to hear?
- make service to his/her institution his/her number one priority ... despite personal sacrifice?
- have a love affair going with his/her organization?
- set a good example in all respects?
- think of the wants and needs of individuals and of their families?
- suffer from "Chicken Littleism"?
- meet the public well?
- get awed by "big wheels," or is he/she at ease with them?
- let concern for his/her "future" govern his/her actions?
- understand the government ... how it works and how to work in it?
- understand Congress and how to work with congressmen?
- express himself/herself well ... on paper and orally?
- understand the organization he/she serves?
- understand his/her institution's role in government and its relations with state and local governments?
- understand his/her institution's role in community and business affairs?
- make things happen?
- get things done?

- lead, not push?
- make a good team with his/her spouse in representing the institution he/she serves?
- have imagination?
- worry about who gets the credit?
- praise his/her people?
- go to bat for his/her people?

WILL THIS PERSON:

- disagree with me when he/she thinks I am wrong?
- stand up and be counted?

CAN THIS PERSON:

- "walk with kings, and not lose the common touch?"
- handle a huge workload and not lose the bubble?
- keep twelve oranges in the air at once and not drop any?
- accept the ideas of others?
- convey his/her ideas to others ... and sell them?
- laugh at himself/herself?
- laugh at all ... i.e., does he/she have a good sense of humor?
- deal with the press and other media?
- walk in the other person's shoes, no matter how big or small?
- make a speech that people will listen to?
- sort out problems and keep his/her priorities straight?

- hit a golf ball in a shower stall and not get beaned?
- think on his/her feet?
- be tough when necessary?
- take an unpopular, but necessary, stand and stick to it?
- grasp new concepts quickly?
- identify problems (vs. symptoms) ... and get them solved?
- find a new course if the one he/she has selected comes a-cropper ... or does he/she get "lost" in the infamous, single-tree "impenetrable forest"?
- make decisions? does he/she make them?
- handle pressure?
- inspire others?

WOULD I WANT TO WORK WITH THIS PERSON AS A FELLOW LEADER?

HAS THIS PERSON GOT "CLASS"?

p. *"antenna" checklist*   It is important for all leaders to stay "tuned in" to patterns of activities of their organizations, to be open to feedback and to criticism, and to listen to their subordinate leaders. This checklist can be helpful to leaders who wish to stay in touch over the entire period of their leadership.

- Unethical phrases to listen for:
    - —pencil whipping
    - —fudging the figures
    - —cooking the numbers
    - —gaming the program
    - —bending the facts
    - —manipulating the data

- Careerist phrases to listen for:
    - —"I don't trust the personnel system."
    - —"Who is your sponsor?"
    - —"I don't have a sponsor."
    - —"You need to get on board."
    - —"I need to get my ticket punched."
    - —"It's not what you know, it's who you know."
    - —"I need some face-time with the boss."
    - —"I want a high visibility job."
    - —"Joe 'talks a good game.' "
    - —"To get ahead you have got to go along."
    - —"You need to quit 'fighting the problem.' "
    - —"Be careful—the boss likes to 'shoot the messenger.' "

- Signals indicating the Peter (or Paul) Principle is at work:
    - —"It sure takes X a long time to get something done."

—"Why can't X seem to focus in on the issue?"

—"I can never get Z to take a position on anything."

—"Have you noticed that X is always defensive?"

—"Y has no initiative."

—"Z has lost his drive."

—"X was a great staff officer, but seems lost as a leader."

—"Y's folks are afraid of him."

—"Z's people are frustrated."

—"X has a bad case of 'not invented here.' "

—"Y seems to complain all the time."

—"Z is on the road a lot—I wonder who is minding the store?"

—"X never seems to make any deadlines."

—"Is that job too big for Y?"

—"Z is out of touch."

—"How come X surrounds himself with cronies?"

—"Y has no sense of outrage."

—"Z lets the system screw over his people."

q. *phrases to avoid checklist*

- "Make it happen now."
  —This statement by a leader often leads to someone on the staff cutting corners to the point of violation of personal or institutional integrity, and possibly leads to decisions that are not well coordinated, thoughtful, or in accordance with established priorities.
- "I don't get mad—I get even."
  —This is an intimidating statement which lacks dignity, and which creates a climate of fear throughout an organization.
- "I don't like surprises."
  —This commonly used phrase seems reasonably benign, and useful, but it often leads to many decisions being pushed up too high—an impediment to innovation and initiative on the part of subordinate commanders and staff officials.
- "My door is always open."
  —This overused phrase is often misleading or wrong. A leader of a large organization who always has his door open to his subordinates at all levels often becomes buried in minutiae. The leader who says his door is always open when it is not will soon find he has created an atmosphere of cynicism and skepticism about his availability to subordinates.
- "Be sure to keep me informed."
  —This is a sure-fire way to ensure an overly full in-box and lots of phone calls, both day and night. The phrase is the antithesis of delegation and empowerment of subordinates which are two key principles in leading large and complex organizations.

- "We can't handle any new initiatives this year."

    —This kind of guidance is counterproductive to taking an organization to higher levels of good planning, competence, and efficiency. The leader who cuts off new initiatives because of budgetary or other reasons may be making a major mistake. If he is actively engaged in divestiture activities to unload organizations, weapon systems, missions, manpower, etc., that are no longer needed, he ought to be able to develop, encourage, and implement new initiatives every year.

- "If it ain't broke, don't fix it."

    —This commonly used phrase seems to make a great deal of sense, but, in fact, is often an impediment to progress in an organization. Just because an organization is running well does not mean that innovation, new ideas, and new initiatives aren't helpful. If "it" is not broken, you should not fix it, but, on the other hand, if "it" is not broken, it still might be improved incrementally with initiative and new ideas.

- "My mind is closed on that issue."

    —This is an unwise phrase on two counts: A leader's mind should never be totally closed on any issue since changing circumstances or new data may require a readdressal of issues. The phrase sends a signal of great rigidity. Leaders should remind themselves to avoid being like the colonel in *The Bridge on the River Kwai*—it was right to build the bridge, but, later, it was just as right to destroy it.

r. *congressional visit checklist*   This checklist provides guidelines to be considered by a leader when a member of Congress or a staff member from Congress is coming to visit an organization. The items here do not necessarily require action but will remind the leader of those areas that he might wish to review or have his staff investigate prior to the congressional visit.

- Are you aware of the rights of congressional members; of the sense, the direction of the Congress in session?
  - —Congress is not the enemy
  - —members have a right to ask questions
  - —members and their questions deserve your timely response
  - —it is important to know the current issues and emphases of Congress
- Are you aware of the significance of the constituents and constituent interest?
  - —consider providing opportunities for members of Congress to meet constituents
  - —minimize briefings to members
  - —provide a list of people the member met
  - —emphasize women and minorities participation in your mission
- Are you aware that it may be necessary to treat members and staffers differently?
  - —personal staffers manage the member's office
  - —professional staffers work directly on legislation
  - —staffers can be very influential with their member

—staffers are issue-oriented; they want detail
  —be truthful and objective
  —remember that briefings to staffers can be more lengthy than those to the member
  —provide point papers and copies of charts
  —have experts at your briefings to brief and to answer questions
  —keep the number of your people at the briefings small
—members tend to be generalists, more interested in orientation than in details
  —make briefings few and short
  —provide overview of mission
  —speak in layman's terms; avoid acronyms
  —give windshield and walking tours
  —provide hands-on demonstrations
—members are usually interested in meeting constituents
—members look to the uniform for expertise

• Are you well aware of the issues to be discussed?
  —know primary versus secondary issues
  —know your agenda versus the agency, service, or institution; the institutional agenda normally has higher priority
  —know the Washington agenda
  —know institutional priorities on issues
  —know the various sides of the issues
  —show things in a balanced way

- Are you aware that your attitude is all-important to a successful visit?
    - —be careful to avoid personality conflicts
    - —be responsive
    - —remain non-partisan
    - —don't try to "snow" anybody
    - —be candid and honest
    - —caveat personal opinions
    - —don't shoot from the hip
    - —know the politics of the district/state
    - —put yourself in the member's shoes
    - —be careful in advancing your own agenda
    - —be enthusiastic and positive
- Have you coordinated the visit with appropriate agencies?
    - —rely on legislative liaison for guidance
    - —obtain background information from higher headquarters or legislative liaison at the Pentagon
    - —use Guard/Reserve personnel as information sources on the visitor, if appropriate
    - —get local civilians involved; cultivate their support continually
    - —ensure functional area coordination between your unit and higher headquarters
    - —let higher headquarters know how the visit went; relate any unplanned incident or major mistakes you may have made

This checklist is a modification of one that was prepared by two students of the Class of 1986 of the National War College: Lieutenant Colonel Wilson R. Rutherford, III, US Army, and Lieutenant Colonel Leslie F. Kenne, US Air Force.

APPENDIX B
case studies

1.   You are the head of a large maintenance organization. There are 1,600 people working for you. One of your four subordinate leaders (squadron commanders) has shown indications of having considerable problems in working cooperatively with fellow squadron commanders. In addition, you have observed that in the afternoons the commander's speech is sometimes slurred. The commander seems to be using breath mints a great deal in the afternoons. You suspect that he may be drinking heavily at noontime and that he may have a drinking problem or be an alcoholic. You have no direct evidence or information and the squadron seems to be "protecting" him. As his immediate boss, what do you do?

2.   You are a numbered Air Force commander in Europe and you have five Tactical Fighter, Tactical Reconnaissance, and Tactical Control Wings under your command. The wings have from 4,000–7,000

people and each wing is commanded by a colonel. One of the wing commanders has recently been promoted to general officer and will be leaving shortly. The vice wing commander of this wing is very well qualified, has been in the wing for two years and is the logical choice to move up to become the commander. You have heard informally that the vice wing commander's wife has psychiatric problems which are causing morale problems among the wives of the officers in the wing. (For instance, she has been heard to say to wives of young officers, "I'll have your husband fired.") However, the vice commander refuses to acknowledge that his wife needs psychiatric care. What do you do?

3.   You are a commander of an overseas base and an interbase championship football game is scheduled to take place the next day. It has been raining for four days straight and the field is saturated with water. The skies then clear and the head of your sports program recommends that a helicopter which is temporarily on the base be used to dry out the field by hovering over it for two to three hours that afternoon. The helicopter belongs to another unit and you know the commander of that unit well. What do you do?

4.   You are a senior staff officer on an international military staff. You have a very bright lieutenant colonel (general staff officer) who is a "deluxe" lieutenant colonel, which means he has a promising future in his air force. In another office, you have a talented officer (colonel) from another nation. These two individuals have major personality differences that often lead to shouting matches. What do you do?

5. You are a wing commander of an overseas fighter wing and in the last few months you have lost three F–15 aircraft to accidents and one pilot has been killed. Morale in the wing is low as a result and the wing has lost some confidence in itself. The Chief of Maintenance comes forward to you with a proposal that the wing attempt to establish a new all-time record for sortie production in a 24-hour period by flying 450 individual aircraft flights in a single day. The record for a fighter wing in Europe is 296 sorties. Available to fly are 60 aircraft and 70 pilots. What do you do?

6. You are a commander of a large operational unit. You are having a counselling session with a chief chaplain on your base. After explaining all the fine contributions he has made to the large chapel program, you make a couple of modest criticisms of his programs, including chapel administration and the choir program. Both you and the chaplain are full colonels with approximately the same amount of service. He reacts very negatively and emotionally to your criticism and feels that you are wrong on both counts. What do you do?

7. You are the Director of Plans of one of the military Services stationed in the Pentagon and there are a large number of officers who wish to serve in the Directorate of Plans. As a result it is quite common for you to get letters from interested officers and, on occasion, to get a letter or phone call from a general officer recommending an individual. Over a period of about a month you receive separate letters from seven individual generals recommending a lieuten-

ant colonel to come to work for you. Do you hire him?

8.   You are commander of a large operational unit in an overseas base and the local police as well as your base security police have uncovered a marijuana ring which includes a number of high school students who are selling marijuana to their high school friends. One of the drug salesmen is a son of a colonel who works directly for you. The other drug pushers are the sons of more junior officers and NCOs. What do you do?

9.   You are a British Air Marshal (3-star) who commands both the Royal Air Force in Germany and the Second Allied Tactical Air Force. The four-nation Allied Tactical Air Force (British, Belgian, Dutch, German) is about to expand by one nation as the USAF joins the ATAF. The US commits 2½ tactical wings to the ATAF and sends to the headquarters 35 officers and NCOs, including one brigadier general. Among the nations of the ATAF there is some concern that the Americans will try to dominate the headquarters and will try to impose their doctrine and their life-style on the Allied Tactical Air Force Headquarters. The Americans will be arriving the next day. What do you do?

10.   You are a wing commander in an overseas base in Germany and every three months you meet with the *Burgermeister* (mayor) of the nearby town, the *Landrat* (county commissioner), and with the collective mayor for the 50 small villages in the local area. There are two issues on the agenda for the next meeting. The Germans are very concerned about the increase of aircraft noise, both day and night, in the

local area and you are concerned about the German druggists selling weight control pills with a high amphetamine level which in blood and urine tests cause your personnel to read "positive." How do you approach both of these issues?

11. You are a commander at a military post with a very active and successful interbase and intramural sports program. You go to almost all of the sporting events that are held at your base, including all the interpost football games. In recent games you have noticed thirty or forty of your enlisted personnel drinking heavily and dreaming up obscene cheers to taunt the opposition as well as engaging in shoving matches with each other that once or twice have broken out into fist fights. What do you do?

12. You are a wing commander of a fighter wing on an overseas base and there is a great deal of interest in the press, both international and domestic, about the new airplane your wing has just received. It is your responsibility to host, brief, and answer questions from all the major American TV news media as well as the international and domestic print media throughout Europe and the United States. In one of the questions you receive, a reporter from a major US newspaper asks you your opinion on the sale of this aircraft to a state in the Middle East. How do you answer the question?

13. You are the Commandant of a senior Service college and you have just received a letter from a US ambassador complaining about various students on the overseas trips who were drinking excessively at a social function and, in another case, about a student who missed a day of briefings because he

chose to be with his wife. In a third case, a student brought his girl friend, unannounced, to one of the embassy parties in honor of the students. Due to the desires of many of the embassies to reduce the support burdens—transportation, luggage, space, etc.—the policy was clear that spouses and friends should not accompany, or join, students—or faculty—on any of the trips. What action do you take?

14. You are a general officer in charge of a large staff organization in the Pentagon visiting a major city in the Midwest. You have been asked by the Vice Chief of Staff of your Service to have a session with the editorial board of the major morning newspaper of this city. In the discussion one of the journalists presses you hard about why your Service is not developing a weapon system to accomplish an important mission. You know of a program that, in fact, addresses that mission very well, but the technology is so sensitive that the whole program is highly classified and compartmentalized. How would you handle this line of questioning?

15. As a general officer, you are testifying on Capitol Hill. Just before you leave the Pentagon, you learn of a major testing failure of the weapon system on which you are about to testify. You know the upcoming vote in the committee later that day will be very close. You are getting conflicting advice from your staff. You are quite sure that none of the committee members or the Congressional staff members are aware of the test failure. In your testimony, should you raise the issue of the test failure? If so, what do you say?

16. You are commander of a large ship in the United States Navy. You receive a call from the wife of one of the officers on your ship. She tells you that a "contract" has been arranged and a certain officer on the ship will soon be murdered. The telephone caller had overheard a telephone conversation between her next-door neighbor and someone else. It was clear that the next-door neighbor was setting up an arrangement to have her husband killed in order to collect his insurance money; she has already given the two "hit" men a down payment by check. The wife who was calling you seems to have rather detailed information on where and when the murder will take place. What do you do?

17. You are Chief of Maintenance of an overseas wing and some of your airplanes are on temporary duty for gunnery practice at Zaragosa Air Base in Spain. Airlift aircraft periodically fly to Spain to rotate maintenance men and spare parts. A lieutenant who works for you has just been accused (by a staff sergeant) of shipping an automobile engine for his British-made sports car which is in Zaragosa. The engine was shipped in a large box labeled F–4 parts. What do you do?

18. You are the Deputy Wing Commander for Maintenance in a fighter wing in Europe. After you have been in your position for a few weeks you uncover the fact that your midnight shift has been submitting a daily report at 3:00 AM to higher headquarters showing more aircraft in operationally ready status than are in that status at that hour. When you question this practice you are told that this has been going on for some time. It helps the

wing and the wing commander look good to higher headquarters. Normally by 7:00 AM that number of operationally ready airplanes to maintain the wing at a fully operational ready status are, in fact, available for training (or combat) missions. What do you do?

19.   You are a wing commander at an overseas base and within the next few months you expect a major inspection by both the NATO Tactical Evaluation Team (consisting of officers and NCOs from six of the NATO nations) and the US Air Force inspection team. Many of your squadron commanders are already passing out the word that when dealing with inspectors, one should never raise an issue that might make the wing look bad and should always answer inspectors' questions with answers that make the wing look good. As a wing commander you are uncomfortable with this guidance and feel that everyone in the wing should feel free to "tell it like it is." What do you do?

20.   You are a commander of a large unit in Europe. One morning on the police blotter you notice that a technical sergeant has been picked up for drunken driving at the main gate (driving erratically and having odor of alcohol on his breath). A week later the police blotter reports the blood test "positive" for amphetamines but no trace of alcohol. What do you do?

APPENDIX C
analysis of case studies

The following paragraphs outline the action that was taken for each of the case studies highlighted in Appendix B. A brief discussion will cover what action was taken by the leader. That discussion will be followed, in some cases, by a brief analysis of the strengths and weaknesses of the solution picked by the leader to handle this problem, as well as lessons learned from this experience. All of these events occurred; in some cases, the circumstances have been modified slightly to avoid embarrassing anyone.

1. The individual clearly had a problem, but for some months he was so careful and so secretive about his drinking problem that it was hard to pinpoint specific incidents where he was drinking or drunk on the job. A captain who was the squadron commander's administrative officer was called in by the leader. She was told that her squadron

commander may be an alcoholic; yet, the leader couldn't put his finger on it and needed her to track his behavior and his whereabouts. She agreed to do this. For the next month or two she was able to keep a record, just for the use of the leader, showing where the squadron commander was and when and where he showed signs of drinking during the day. She brought the report back to the leader; it showed clearly that the squadron commander was drinking heavily at noontime. Sometimes he would not return to work or, if he did return, he would close his door and would conduct no business in the afternoon but would sit quietly in his office. After receiving this report from the captain, the leader called in the squadron commander at mid-afternoon.

The leader told the squadron commander that he thought he had a drinking problem; the leader told him to go immediately to the hospital commander to take a blood test to see what his blood-alcohol level was and to get advice and counsel from the medical specialists in the hospital. The blood tests showed that although he had a very low level of alcohol in his blood, he did have liver damage and was clearly a man suffering from alcohol abuse. He was sent to an alcohol rehabilitation program at a hospital one hundred miles away. After four weeks he returned to his position as squadron commander and retained his command until he was reassigned to the United States a few months later.

The involvement of a young captain who worked directly for the squadron commander was probably inappropriate; the leader himself (or his deputy) should have tracked the activities of his subordinate squadron commander. Sending the commander to alcohol rehabilitation and leaving him in his position as squadron commander after rehabilitation was an appropriate action. Alcoholism is a disease and it was important for the squadron commander's self-esteem and for the self-esteem of other people who might be suffering from drinking problems to realize that there is no punishment involved in the treatment of people with alcohol problems. The second mistake the leader made was taking many months to figure out the squadron commander had a problem. If the previous commander had alerted the present commander to this problem during the transition phase, the problem could have been addressed much sooner.

2. Here is a case in which an Air Force two-star general received many indications that a vice commander's wife, because of psychiatric illness, was creating morale problems among the junior officers and their wives in the wing. The vice wing commander was not selected to become a wing commander. He returned to the United States and retired shortly thereafter. The mistake made in this case was that the numbered Air Force commander did not talk to the wing commander on the scene; he could have received some good advice from that individual. Rather than rejecting a well qualified man, the Air Force commander might have given the vice wing commander an opportunity to command the wing on a probationary basis, if he agreed to have his wife seek psychiatric care, or perhaps return to the States. This was a judgment call; since there were so many people who were well qualified to be wing

gÇï

ê The correct answer

commanders, the problem with the spouse was apparently enough to cause the general to choose someone else.

3. The wing commander called his fellow wing commander and asked that the helicopter be used for hovering. The other wing commander, who commanded the helicopter unit, agreed. The helicopter hovered for two or three hours and dried out the field. Within a few weeks, a letter came in from the Air Force headquarters saying that a US Senator had asked, in writing, if the helicopter had been used inappropriately to dry out a football field rather than to conduct regular training exercises. A general officer investigated the situation and recommended reprimands for both wing commanders; the reprimands were issued by the theater commander. The lesson here is clear. Whenever you make decisions relating to the use of government equipment, government aircraft, etc., in unusual ways, you should ask these questions: "Is this a wise thing to do? Is this a legal thing to do? Is this a good way to spend government funds? How would it look in a newspaper column? Or, how would it sound if you had to justify this while testifying on Capitol Hill?" The wing commanders from both bases had no previous experience in Washington and were perhaps not as sensitive to these concerns as they might have been if they had had that experience.

4. The two officers were called in individually and talked to about their differences of views and the antagonism that had built up between them. Both agreed to work on the problem, although both felt that the other individual was to blame. In this case

antagonisms cut across national cultures. In addition, the two individuals had differing philosophies on warfighting and were both very strong personalities. Counselling sessions by the leader seemed to do some good. The fact that the leader was concerned and told the two officers he would be watching the developments in the future seemed to reduce the amount of tension and the amount of problems. The lesson learned here was the importance of uncovering the problem and taking action early, before too much blood was spilled.

5. In this case it was clear that a morale boosting exercise would be very helpful to both the maintenance people and the pilots. The commander set some general guidelines: meaningful training must take place on every sortie; safety had to be a primary concern and the whole exercise must be carefully planned and executed. The chief of maintenance and the director of operations sat down and came up with a reasonable number of sorties for a 24-hour day. After some coordination and debate, it was agreed that 325 sorties would be the goal. Each of the pilots who were scheduled for daytime flights were limited to a maximum of six sorties; the night pilots were limited to a maximum of four sorties. It turned out to be an extraordinary day that boosted morale, particularly on the part of the maintenance people, who were very motivated by the fact that the airplanes were flying a lot and doing well. The maintenance people were absolutely delighted when, at the end of the day, the wing ran out of pilots in the twenty-second hour, had flown 322 sorties, and yet there were 49 aircraft still "mission

capable" and ready to fly. There were no accidents or incidents during the entire day and very few mistakes were made. If there is a lesson to be learned from this it is that setting meaningful records is a very useful motivational tool. It also proves to people that they can do more than they thought they could—a valuable lesson for a combat unit.

6. This experience was very difficult because, despite all the soothing language of the leader, the chaplain blew up. The leader was never able to convince the chaplain that the leader had raised a legitimate point or two in their discussions. It turned out that the chaplain was extremely sensitive to criticism and was not able to weigh objectively constructive criticism. Later, quiet checking on the part of the leader revealed that the chaplain had problems in productively relating to the other chaplains and the non-commissioned officers in the Chaplain's office. The counselling session had uncovered a part of his personality of which the leader had not been aware. The lesson here is that a leader should not be afraid to criticize; criticism may uncover more than you might expect.

7. Clearly, this individual was spending a great deal of his time working on his own future assignment in a very ambitious and "careerist" way by asking all those generals to go to bat for him all at the same time. As a result, he was clearly not spending a great deal of his time concentrating on his present job. All the generals were sent letters by the leader thanking them for their interest, but all were informed that the individual had not been selected to work in the Directorate of Plans. The lesson learned

from this case is that those individuals who are so interested in getting just the right assignment sometimes "shoot themselves in the foot" by coming across as being hyperambitious and unwilling to allow the personnel system to weigh the needs and desires of both the organization and the individual in finding appropriate assignments. Hyperambition hurts many very talented people; leaders should occasionally caution their subordinates, collectively and, when appropriate, individually, about not getting caught in the trap of careerism.

8. In this case, the colonel was confronted directly in order to find out the background of the situation and what he would be willing to do about it. The colonel was quite cavalier about it and felt that it was not that big a problem and that lots of kids were "doing drugs." The son, as well as the father and mother, were sent by the commander through drug rehabilitation in order to ensure that they fully understood the consequences of drug involvement. If the colonel had not been willing to attend drug rehabilitation with his son, and had not been willing to discipline his son, the son would have been sent home with the son's authorization to be in the overseas area discontinued. The colonel, himself, may have been sent home if he had not been willing to take action to end this very unhappy situation. The lesson here is that it doesn't matter what rank you are, there will be opportunities for the children, wives, and family members of senior people to get in trouble with drugs, theft, vandalism, and so forth. It is important for a leader to make it clear that major subordinate leaders have an even greater

responsibility than others to set and maintain high standards for themselves and for members of their families. Top leaders must be "squeaky clean."

9. In this case the British 3-star Air Marshal did some very good and very helpful things. He welcomed the Americans with great warmth and, for the next few weeks, whenever he had the opportunity, both in social and official events or ceremonies, he would make a speech about what a great contribution the Americans would make to the new headquarters and how happy he was to have the American officers and enlisted people and their families here to support the mission. He also gave priority in housing to the new Americans coming to the base so that they could move into housing very quickly. He made special dispensation as far as the schooling situation was concerned so that the Americans could have full access to the British school system on the base. Everything was done with style by the British commander. Although there were a number of British lower ranking people, both officer and enlisted, who felt that Americans coming to this new base was a big mistake, it was clear that the leader did the best possible job to make the Americans feel welcome and to make the people from other NATO nations understand that they were to be welcomed as friends, colleagues, and contributors to the common defense of the Alliance.

10. Fortunately, there was a good meeting of the minds on both sides. American concerns about the drugs and German concerns about the noise were frankly discussed. The *Burgermeister* agreed to approach all the druggists and pharmacists in the area

to explain the problem and to ask them to be very careful about dispensing drugs to Americans, particularly certain types of drugs with a high amphetamine content. In addition, the druggists were asked to report on anyone buying these kinds of drugs in large quantities. The American commander made a pledge to continue to have the F–15's take off without engaging the noisy engine afterburner. He also agreed to reduce the amount of flying in the evenings and on the weekends as much as possible, and to talk to sister wing commanders to make sure that they fully understood the concerns of the people in the area about low level flying and very high noise levels. The American leader also was able to report to the mayor that measurements of the noise factors by an authoritative German survey group had been accomplished and that they had reported that the noise around the Bitburg air base was lower than most bases elsewhere in Germany. This helped ease the concern of the *Burgermeister* considerably. It also gave him a good set of facts to take back to his constituents.

11. The leader approached these individuals, sat down among them and began to talk to them in a friendly way. He let them know that he was interested in their having a good time but that he would be with them for the rest of the game. It soon became clear that they were willing to be more careful about what they said and what they did. The fact that some of them knew what the leader had written in the base newspaper about decorum and conduct at football games helped. The leader later wrote additional articles in the base newspaper on this

subject. Although the problem did not completely go away, it did diminish during the rest of the season. The lesson learned here is that whenever you have a large number of people congregating at a sporting event, there is always the possibility of too much drinking or the harassment of the other team, its cheerleaders, or its fans. The commander or subordinate commanders should attend major sporting events and intervene diplomatically but firmly in any situation that looks like it is beginning to get out of hand. It is also useful in identifying certain troublemakers so they can be subsequently disciplined.

12. In this case, the wing commander answered that he was opposed to the sale of F–15's. He said that you have to be careful to whom you sell your airplanes because one day the people who receive those airplanes may be your enemies. The article appeared in the *Atlanta Constitution* and was read by President Carter within a few days. It caused embarrassment to the Air Force and the wing commander. The question should probably have been answered along the following lines, "That is a policy issue that is made in Washington after due consideration of all factors. As wing commander in Europe, I do not have all the facts to be able to make a statement as to the wisdom of this particular decision in the Middle East. I would defer to the DOD and State Department spokesmen to answer that question."

13. This is a composite of a number of factors that have come to play at the joint senior Service colleges in the last few years. Basically, what the Commandant needs to do in all subsequent classes is to ensure that the ground rules are well established for

overseas trips. He needs to explain that spouses and friends are not permitted to go for a number of good reasons, that students and faculty are expected to attend all scheduled events and that they are expected to be prudent about drinking. If there is someone with a drinking problem, the trip leader should make sure this individual does not embarrass himself, the War College, or the nation. Even though people at the War Colleges are highly selected people, a few will have problems. One College recently had to dismiss an individual who had been dishonest in filling out his personnel record. Problems of alcoholism occur from time to time. A number of serious family health problems as well as an occasional difficult divorce situation occur. It is important for a commander to be on top of these issues, to help people in need, to be empathetic with the problems of subordinates and, first and foremost, to live up to the organization's standards. That way, the organization will stay on an even keel, and although there will be an occasional setback or embarrassment, it will be the exception rather than the rule.

In these specific cases, the Commandant made note of these clear violations of well-articulated policy in the students' final training report. Since attendance at a joint senior Service college is such a rare privilege, poor performance or violations of policy by students should become part of the official record.

14. You are in a very delicate area here. It is important to be forthright with the media while, at the same time, guarding very sensitive and highly classified information. The General answered it in the

following way: "This is an area that we have great concern about and we are pursuing a number of technological solutions in hopes of developing a weapon system that will fill this gap." If the reporter continues to press for information, the best approach is probably to follow up by saying that "These technologies are of such a sensitive nature that it would be inappropriate for me to comment further on the specifics."

15. The General should and did raise this issue and gave as much information to the committee as he had available on the test failure. He did this for a number of reasons. First, it would be wrong to withhold important information from a duly constituted congressional committee. Second, by withholding information, the General takes the considerable risk of losing credibility and trust. At a later point, committee members and staffers might learn that there was a failure and that the General had some information about it prior to his testimony that day. It is important to realize that the movement of a program through the Congress is a long and complex process that continues over a number of years. There are lots of opportunities for the Congress to withhold funds or cancel the program. A short-term victory often leads to a long-term defeat if the victory is gained through manipulation of the facts or withholding of information. Members of Congress and congressional staffers have long memories, and individuals who testify on Capitol Hill should realize that their most important assets are credibility and truth.

16. The Commander called in a small group of his staff, as well as the FBI, to do some preliminary in-

vestigation of this situation and to give the Commander advice. When it became clear that the facts substantiated the information of the telephone caller, the Commander called in the officer and quietly laid out the situation to him. Although the officer initially did not believe the Commander, when all the facts were known he changed his mind. The FBI set a trap and the officer went to the spot where the murder was to take place. The two men were apprehended and all three individuals, including the officer's wife, were indicted for, and convicted of, attempted murder and sent to jail.

17. After the Commander ascertained the facts of this situation he called in the lieutenant and asked him for his side of the story. The lieutenant readily admitted that he had done what he had been accused of doing, but indicated that he saw no other option for getting the engine to Spain. As the airplane was only half full, and he had drained the engine of all fuel and oil, he felt he had done nothing wrong. The Commander pointed out to him the integrity issue involved and had an opportunity to emphasize the importance of maintaining high integrity as a professional officer. The Commander gave the lieutenant a letter of reprimand, but removed it from his file at a later point because the Commander felt the lieutenant had learned a lesson from the event and the Commander did not wish to do permanent damage to the young officer's career.

18. The Deputy Wing Commander for Maintenance approached the Wing Commander the next day and explained quite bluntly that the Wing was sending a false and misleading official report to higher head-

quarters and to the JCS. He explained to the Wing Commander that he thought this was wrong, and in addition, that it was not in the interest of the Wing. By reporting accurately, there was a better chance of getting supply and manpower support to solve the underlying problem of low readiness. He suggested to the Wing Commander that, starting the next morning, the report be made honestly and that the Wing Commander call the higher headquarters to let them know why the readiness status would be dropping so dramatically. The Wing Commander readily agreed. The Deputy Wing Commander for Maintenance then called a meeting of his senior maintenance team (both officers and noncommissioned officers). He explained to them that it was wrong, and was not in the interest of the maintenance organization of the Wing or the Wing Commander, to overstate combat capability. The nice thing about this story was there was no objection on the part of either the Wing Commander or the maintenance leaders to returning to a system of honest reporting.

19. In the next issue of the weekly base newspaper the Commander wrote an article outlining the fact that he wanted all the members of the Wing to answer the questions of the inspectors honestly and to withhold no important information. He indicated that he wanted them to surface their problems so that the inspectors would understand that they knew where their problems were and that they were working on them. Fortunately, the philosophy of the major Command was that units would get higher marks if they were willing to admit to the inspectors where their problems were rather than hide

them from the inspectors or withhold information. In the inspection that took place shortly thereafter, the Wing received very high marks and was specifically complimented in the preface to the inspection report for being aware of the problem areas and being willing to discuss them candidly with the inspection team members.

20. The Commander called in his Chief of Security Police and his Hospital Commander and told them that he thought something was strange. He asked them to investigate the situation to try to determine why someone with alcohol on his breath showed no alcohol in his blood. A few days later the Hospital Commander and Security Chief returned to outline the results of their investigation. The technical sergeant, having been driven home by the security police after the blood alcohol test, approached his next-door neighbor, who was also a sergeant. He told his neighbor that he was very concerned about losing his license for a year as a result of driving while intoxicated. He was also concerned that his wife, who did not drive, would have no way to get to work. The next-door neighbor suggested that both individuals go to the hospital that night and see if they could negotiate a blood swapping deal with the medical corpsman at the hospital. They were able to do that, but the next-door neighbor failed to mention that he had been using amphetamines. In this case, disciplinary action was taken against all three individuals involved in this scam. Mistakes that were made, however, were the following: the Wing Commander failed to call in the technical sergeant's Squadron Commander; in addition, the Squadron

Commander, the Hospital Commander, and the Chief of Security Police all failed to note the discrepancy, on the police blotter, in the blood alcohol test when the results became known. The major lesson here is that the police blotter will tell you a lot if it is read carefully by the commander and the subordinate commanders.

SELECTED BIBLIOGRAPHY

The literature on leadership is rich and diverse. Those individuals interested in reading in the area of leadership are often at a loss finding the books that are the most relevant to the leadership challenges and opportunities facing them. This bibliography highlights those books which would be particularly helpful to leaders of large and complex organizations and, more specifically, those leaders in the public sector: in government, and in the military.

James McGregor Burns, *Leadership*, Harper and Row, New York, 1978.

- This Pulitzer Prize and National Book Award winning book concentrates on political leadership. Burns' discussion of transactional and transforming leadership is tremendously insightful. Because of the conceptual nature of the book, it makes heavy reading, and for those readers who don't have time to read the entire work, I recommend those portions which focus on transforming leadership.

Edmond Morris, *The Rise of Theodore Roosevelt*, Coward, McCann, and Geoghegan, Inc., New York, 1979.

- This elegant and insightful political biography gives insights into the maturation and intellectual development of one of America's greatest leaders. Readers who dive into this book will quickly understand why President Reagan chose Morris to be his biographer and has given him personal access to the White House during Reagan's last three years in office.

John Wareham, *Secrets of a Corporate Headhunter*, Atheneum Press, New York, 1980.

- This analysis of leadership from the unique perspective of a headhunter provides a kind of "street smart," "gloves off" perspective. Particularly insightful is Chapter Eight, "How to Fire and Still Be Friends."

Tom Peters and Nancy Austin, *A Passion for Excellence: The Leadership Difference*, Random House, New York, 1985.

- An up-to-date study of leadership in the business world. The first and last parts of this book are particularly recommended.

Robert L. Taylor and William E. Rosenbach, eds., *Military Leadership: In Pursuit of Excellence*, Westview Press, Boulder, Colorado, 1984.

- In my opinion, the best collection of useful articles on military leadership that is available. Chapters that are particularly recommended are by James Stokesbury, General Matthew Ridgway, General S. L. A. Marshall, Colonel Malham Wakin, Admiral James Stockdale, and Thomas Cronin.

Norman F. Dixon, *On the Psychology of Military Incompetence*, Basic Books, New York, 1976.
- This book by a British author examines military incompetence from a European perspective. By the use of case studies, and careful analysis, Dixon demonstrates quite conclusively the dysfunctional aspects of authoritarian leadership in combat environments.

Sun Tzu, *The Art of War*, Oxford University Press, London, 1963 (translation by Samuel B. Griffith).
- Generally considered the best book on strategy ever written. Pages 114–115 and 128–129 are particularly recommended.

Karl Von Clausewitz, *On War*, Princeton University Press, Princeton, NJ, 1976 (translation by Michael Howard and Peter Paret).
- This classic on strategy has a particularly insightful chapter on military genius (pages 100–112) which should be mandatory reading for all students of leadership.

Kenneth Blanchard and Spencer Johnson, *The One-Minute Manager*, William Morrow and Company, New York, 1982.
- This short book is a quick read but has some useful insights into the value of delegation.

Forrest Pogue, *George C. Marshall,* 4 vols., Viking Press, New York, 1963, 1966, 1973, forthcoming.
- This four-volume series (three volumes have been published and the fourth is forthcoming) is the finest biography of an American military leader available in the literature. Volumes two and three are particularly recommended. These volumes discuss Marshall's leadership in the immediate prewar period and during World War II.

Kent Roberts Greenfield, *Command Decisions,* Center of Military History, Washington, DC, 1960.
- This collection of studies by a number of eminent historians examines key decisions by American, German, Japanese, and other national leaders just prior to and during World War II.

Warren Bennis, *Leaders,* Harper and Row, New York, 1985.
- Bennis' insights on the role of the leader in infusing organizations with energy, in creating a culture of pride, in teachership, in the empowerment of subordinate leaders, and in avoiding activities that waste people's time are all quite persuasive. His careful research of many successful business leaders has uncovered an interesting statistic: almost all are happily married to their first wife.

INDEX

THE AUTHOR

Perry Smith has spent his entire life in the military. Born at West Point into an Army family, he first left the country when he was six months old and has traveled extensively ever since. Upon graduation from the United States Military Academy, he chose the Air Force as his career and spent all of his operational years in fighter aviation flying F–100s, F–4s (in combat), and F–15s. He has held leadership positions at many levels, both in the United States and in Europe. He commanded the F–15 Wing at Bitburg, Germany and was the first American general to serve in the Second Allied Tactical Air Force in northern Germany. He served at the Pentagon in a number of positions, including Military Assistant to the Deputy Secretary of Defense and Director of Plans for the Air Force. His teaching experience at the Air Force Academy and the National War College followed the completion of a Ph.D. in International Relations at Columbia University. His dissertation won the Helen Dwight Reed Award from the American Political Science Association. While Commandant of the National War College, he taught a number of courses, including a course on leadership of large organizations. He is the author of *The Air Force Plans for Peace: 1943–1945*, The Johns Hopkins Press, Baltimore, 1970, as well as coauthor for a forthcoming book from NDU Press on national security and long-range planning. Perry Smith retired from the Air Force in 1986.